Françoise Détienne

Software Design – Cognitive Aspects

Translator and Editor: Frank Bott

 Springer

KT-573-524

Francoise Détienne, PhD
Unité de recherche INRIA Rocquencourt,
Domaine de Voluceau, Rocquencourt,
BP 105 – 78153 Le Chesnay Cedex, France

Translator and Editor
Frank Bott, MA, MBCS, CEng
Department of Computer Science
UWA
Penglais
Aberystwyth SY23 3BD

British Library Cataloguing in Publication Data
Detienne, Francoise
    Software design : cognitive aspects. – (Practitioner series)
    1. Computer software – Development. 2. Computer software – Reusability
    I. Title
005.1
ISBN 1852332530

Library of Congress Cataloging-in-Publication Data
Détienne, Francoise.
    Software design – cogitive aspects/Francoise Détienne.
        p. cm. --(Practitioner series)
    Includes bibliographical references and index.
    ISBN 1–85233–253–0 (alk. paper)
    1. Computer software--Development. 2. Computer programming--Psychological aspects.
I. Title. II. Series.

QA76.76.D47 D4775 2001
005.1–dc21

                                                                    2001032057

Practitioner series ISSN 1439–9245

ISBN 1-85233-253-0   Springer-Verlag London Berlin Heidelberg
a member of BertelsmannSpringerScience + Business Media GmbH
http://www.springer.co.uk

Typeset by Florence Production Ltd, Stoodleigh, Devon
Printed and bound by the Athenæum Press Ltd., Gateshead, Tyne and Wear
34/3830-543210 Printed on acid-free paper SPIN 10741909

Springer

London
Berlin
Heidelberg
New York
Barcelona
Hong Kong
Milan
Paris
Singapore
Tokyo

Other titles in this series:

Editorial Foreword

The activities involved in software engineering are among the most intellectually demanding of any that are undertaken by comparatively large groups of people.

Many claims are made for the efficacy and utility of new approaches to software engineering - structured methodologies, new programming paradigms, new tools, and so on. Evidence to support such claims is thin and such evidence as there is, is largely anecdotal. Of proper scientific evidence there is remarkably little. Furthermore, such as there is can be described as 'black box', that is, it demonstrates a correlation between the use of a certain technique and an improvement in some aspect of the development. It does not demonstrate how the technique achieves the observed effect.

On the other hand, research into the psychology of programming and software development more generally has been largely (though not entirely) confined to small scale laboratory experiments. These are generally based on sound experimental design and seek to demonstrate the way in which factors studied achieve the observed effects but they are so far removed from the reality of industrial software engineering that one is forced to question their applicability.

Dr Détienne is one of the most distinguished and prolific researchers working in the field. Her book describes the current state of knowledge in the field of programming psychology and the psychology of software design. It is rather different from the other books in the Practitioner Series in that it is largely concerned with academic research. However, this academic research is of considerable interest to the practitioner. At the very least, it will induce a healthy scepticism towards the claims made for many techniques and tools. It will be of particular interest to software development managers because it addresses directly the cognitive aspects of two currently fashionable silver bullets, object orientation and reuse.

This book was originally intended primarily for readers active in the field of cognitive psychology, with software engineers as a subsidiary readership. With the author's full agreement, I have rearranged some of the material so as to change the emphasis of the book and I have added new material to make the book more relevant to software engineers.

It cannot be a pleasant experience for an author to find her work being mauled in translation to meet the needs of an audience different from the one for which it was originally intended. I would like to record my appreciation of the co-operation and assistance that I received from Dr Détienne throughout this process.

Frank Bott
Translator and editor
For the Editorial Board

Preface

The aim of this book is to present a critical synthesis of research in the field commonly known as the psychology of programming. This covers the activities involved in the different programming[1] tasks, such as analysis, design, coding and maintenance. The purpose of such research is to provide ergonomic recommendations for the specification of development environments and programming languages, as well as training and education aids. More generally, we are interested in providing experts with aids to problem-solving.

Themes

The book is centred around three themes: (1) the design of software, (2) the reuse of software and (3) the understanding of completed software for the purposes of modification, debugging or reuse. More peripherally, we shall address program documentation. We shall call on the theoretical frameworks developed in cognitive psychology for the study of problem solving, reasoning by analogy, and the production and understanding of text.

Cognitive aspects of the use of graphical languages for designing software have been the subject of some recent research (Green and Petre, 1996; Petre, 1995; Petre and Green, 1992, 1993) as has the process of co-operation in collective design (Robillard *et al.*, 1998). It seems to us too soon to be trying to exploit this work in a practical way and we have therefore excluded it from consideration in this book. We have considered experience only peripherally, by taking into account its role in the building of schemas and the transfer of such knowledge during the learning of an *n*'th language.

Structure of the Book

Chapter 1 presents a history of research carried out in the psychology of programming from the mid–70s onwards. We distinguish two periods. The first is characterized by the use of experimental paradigms and by the absence of a theoretical framework. The second notes the emergence of new experimental paradigms and borrows its theoretical frameworks freely from cognitive psychology. The research presented here belongs largely to this second period. If we sometimes cite earlier work, it is to reposition it in an appropriate theoretical framework that will allow the results obtained to be analysed.

---

[1]The term programming is used here in its broad sense and is not limited to coding.

In Chapter 2, we investigate the nature of a computer program, on the one hand from a computational point of view and, on the other hand, from a psychological point of view. Throughout the book we shall be drawing a parallel between studies of the processing (production and understanding) of natural language text and the processing of program text. In this context we shall be looking at two questions: (1) what are the similarities and differences between a computer program and a natural language text and (2) what are the similarities and differences between programming languages and natural language?

The rest of the book deals with two different aspects of programming: the production of programs (Chapters 3, 4 and 5) and the understanding of programs (Chapters 6 and 7).

As far as programming is concerned, we present theoretical approaches to program design in Chapter 3, and to reuse in design in Chapter 4. These theoretical approaches will be evaluated on the basis of the results of empirical studies. The practical implications of this research will be discussed as well as the prospects for further research. More particularly, in Chapter 5 we shall be interested in the effect of one programming paradigm, namely object orientation, on program production activities.

As far as understanding is concerned, in Chapter 6 we present the theoretical approaches to understanding programs. Again we shall evaluate them on the basis of empirical results and discuss the practical implications and the prospects for future research. The effect that the task and the textual structure have on understanding will be developed in Chapter 7.

In Chapter 8, we sum up the contribution of the research in cognitive psychology and then discuss the conditions necessary if the ergonomic implications of the material presented here are really to be taken into account in the field of computing.

Who Is This Book For?

This book is aimed at practitioners, research workers and students in a range of disciplines: computing, especially software engineering, cognitive psychology, and cognitive ergonomics.

Computing Specialists

Computing is both the subject of the research described here and an application area for its results. The results presented thus have an impact on the ergonomic specifications of programming tools, with the goal of improving the compatibility between the tools and their users, the programmers. By tools here, we mean not only programming languages and programming environments but also the programming models developed in software engineering, such as process models and structured methods. Throughout the book we shall emphasize the ergonomic implications of the theoretical approaches presented.

We are hoping to sensitize computer specialists to the psychology of programming and, more generally, to cognitive ergonomics. We have written this book in an attempt to transfer ideas from these fields into the computing community.

Cognitive Psychologists and Ergonomists

The work presented is strongly orientated towards cognitive ergonomics. This orientation is explained by the fact that the activities studied are situational, that is, they form part of a task.

There are many theoretical borrowings from cognitive psychology. Our interest is to test and extend the models coming out of psychology by applying them to situations that involve a number of activities related to realistic and professional tasks. The models borrowed have come out of research into problem solving and into the production and understanding of text. Now, in the programming situation, these activities are determined by the task and the experience of the subjects is an important factor in the situation. Further, the complexity of the situations studied is often greater than that of properly experimental studies. Part of the interest of this work, for the psychologist and the ergonomist, is to analyse how these models can be applied to such complex situations, to discuss their limitations and to open up new paths for research.

Computer programming is a complex field. We have made some effort to present the essential concepts of the field in order to make the book understandable to readers who are not programmers. The chapter that, to us, seems to require more technical knowledge, and perhaps real practical experience, is Chapter 5 on the design and reuse of object-oriented programs. This chapter takes up the theoretical points in Chapters 3 and 4, on the design and reuse of software, and develops them within the framework of object-oriented programming. The reader who is new to programming can ignore Chapter 5 without missing the essential theoretical points of these ideas.

References and Footnotes

In order to avoid cluttering the text, references are, in most cases, indicated by superscript numerals. These refer to lists of authors and dates at the end of each chapter. Full bibliographical references will be found at the end of the book.

Footnotes are indicated by superscript lower case letters.

Contents

1. *Historical Background*

The study of the psychology of programming started in the 1970s[a]. Two distinct periods can be identified. In the first, research was largely in the hands of computer scientists and its main purpose was the evaluation of software tools in terms of performance. This was the period of experimental studies looking to analyse the effect of different factors (such as indentation) on performance in different programming tasks, without cognitive models to take account of the activities in the different tasks. The book that best illustrates the studies of this period is that by Shneiderman (1980); it had some impact on the world of computing when it was first published.

For the last 15 years or so there has been a growing interest in the field on the part of psychologists and ergonomists, who have seen programming as a field in which to study the activities of design, comprehension, and expert problem solving, as well as a means of developing and evaluating tools to help with them. This second period is characterized by the development of cognitive models of programming and by the use of more clinical methods of activity analysis, alongside of, and as a complement to, experimental methods. Researchers in this field of science meet at annual or biannual workshops: that of the Psychology of Programming Interest Group in Europe, and the Empirical Studies of Programmers in North America. These meetings have scientifically been very productive.

1.1 The 1970s

1.1.1 The Experimental Paradigm

The roots of the study of programming lay in computer scientists' interest in testing new programming tools. As programming itself evolved by distancing itself from the use of machine languages, so methods, languages and visualization tools were developed. The need to validate these tools experimentally thus arose. To do this, computer scientists borrowed methods from experimental psychology to evaluate the tools[1]. These experimental methods allow one to test the effect of one or more

---

[a]Hoc *et al.* (1990) place the birth in the 1960s. It is true that a French study (Rouanet and Gateau, 1967) of that period aimed to analyse data processing, but this study was completely unique at the time and we have to wait until the 1970s before further work appears.

1

factors, called independent variables, on the values taken by a dependent variable. The principle is to construct an experimental situation by varying the values of one independent variable. In the simplest case, we have an experimental condition where the variable is present and a control condition where this variable is absent, all other things being the same. One then measures the effect of this variable on the dependent variable, which is, in these studies, usually a performance indicator.

To illustrate this approach, we cite a hypothetical example given by Shneiderman (1980). This is a bi-factorial study, that is, a study involving two factors. The two independent variables whose effect we want to measure are, on the one hand, the use of meaningful mnemonic variable names and, on the other, the use of comments. Each variable may be present or absent. The dependent variable is a measure of performance in modifying a program. Combining these two factors, we obtain four experimental conditions to which one can randomly expose the experimental subjects. It is important that the factor of the subjects' experience is properly controlled in the study, which means that one must be sure that the subjects come from a single population whose characteristics can be described. Table 1.1 shows the hypothetical results of such an experiment.

From the means shown in the last column and the last row, one can see that there is an effect from the factor 'presence of comments' on the one hand, and from the factor 'presence of mnemonic names for variables' on the other.

A second stage is then to carry out statistical tests, of the analysis of variance type (ANOVA), which will allow us to show what is the probability of not finding these results when the experiment is replicated with similar groups. If the probability is small, say one in a thousand for the effect of an independent variable, then one can say that this variable has a significant effect at $p = 0.001$.

As stated above, the dependent variables most commonly used in the studies of this period are performance indicators. These indicators are often related to different programming tasks, for example, in a debugging task, they might be the number of errors detected and corrected, and the time taken to detect them. These indicators measure very clearly success in a given task in terms of the final product of the activity but don't in any sense describe the activity used to accomplish the task. We shall see that this causes a problem in interpreting the results.

Another experimental approach that characterizes the studies of this first period is the search for correlations between, on the one hand, factors belonging to the subject, e.g. the number of years of programming experience, and, on the other

Table 1.1 Mean of the modification scores obtained in a bi-factorial experiment (taken from Shneidermann, 1980, p. 20).

	Variable names		
	Mnemonic	Non-mnemonic	
With comments	84.5	72.3	78.4
Without comments	75.4	56.8	66.1
	80.0	64.6	72.3

hand, behavioural factors, e.g. success in a test supposed to measure the ability to understand programs. The practical objective of such studies was to develop tests of competence for staff selection purposes. It is important to remember, however, that the establishment of a correlation between two factors does not mean that there exists a causal relationship between them.

1.1.2 Methodological Criticism

A number of methodological criticisms can be made of this early work. In practice, it is difficult to isolate a single factor and vary it without inducing other changes in the situation. One can still try to isolate it but at the risk of creating a rather artificial situation. We shall illustrate this methodological limitation through two examples, the first demonstrating, to our way of thinking, a rather amateurish experimental approach, and the second illustrating a more professional approach, but one that creates a relatively artificial situation.

Gannon (1977) studied the effect of typing in a programming language on the performance of a programming design task as measured *inter alia* by the number of errors in the program. The independent variable has two values: 'static typing present' (that is, the type of a variable must be declared before it is used) and 'static typing absent'. In order to change this variable, the author has had to use two different languages. This has the effect of varying not only the factor studied but also many other syntactic and semantic characteristics of the languages. Interpretation of the results is thus difficult because there are other factors, confused with the independent variable, which could also be the cause of the results obtained.

To avoid this methodological problem, some researchers[2] have created micro-languages that vary only in one or a few well-identified factors. They have thus been able to compare the effect of different types of loops (goto, nested, etc.) or different types of test on the performance of different tasks. In doing this, they create a rather artificial situation in comparison with the situation in which programming usually takes place. They defend their position by stating

> The technique of using severely restricted micro-languages allows comprehensive conclusions to be reached ... In our opinion, at present more can be lost than learned by increasing the size of the experimental language[3].

Gannon defends the opposite approach, considering that the use of micro-languages is too artificial:

> Language features must be evaluated in the context in which they are used, and creating too small a language may prevent the observation of errors resulting from the interaction of language features[4].

1.1.3 Absence of a Theoretical Framework

Another problem is linked to the absence of a theoretical framework and to the use of performance indicators that measure the final result of the task; this makes it difficult to explain the mechanism of an effect. In fact, these studies offer no explanatory model in terms of cognitive processes for how an effect works. In no case do they explain how and why a variable has an effect on the performance. Further, the absence of an effect on performance has, in our view, very limited value in indicating the effect of the factor under consideration. This effect may exist but just not be detected by the final indicators. In order to detect the effect in such a case we need indicators that bear on the individual activities themselves rather than on the task as a whole. It was only in research of the second period that methods were introduced to analyse the activity in its true sense. We shall give an example that illustrates the methodological limitations of the first period and look forward to the paradigmatic changes that came into use during the second period.

The example again concerns the use of meaningful or non-meaningful names for variables. Recall that a program is made up of predefined symbols (operators, reserved words) and of names chosen by the programmer (names of variables, procedures, etc.). One might expect that the presence of meaningful names in a program will help in understanding it. However, early studies relating to this factor do not always reveal that it has a positive effect on understanding. Weissman (1974) failed to find that the factor had any effect on different programming tasks. Another study (Sheppard, Curtis, Milliman and Love, 1979) failed to find any effect on the ability to reproduce a functionally equivalent program from memory. Shneiderman (1980) showed that the more complex the program, the more the use of mnemonic variable names helps understanding, measured by the error detection rate in a debugging task. Although some of this work allows us to understand better under what conditions an effect of this variable can be observed in terms of comprehension performance, it does not show what cognitive mechanisms are at work.

Researchers studying program understanding in the second period built themselves theoretical frameworks and corresponding experimental paradigms. Thus one might hypothesize that a meaningful name is a semantic index that allows for a knowledge structure (in this case a variable schema) stored in long-term memory to be activated and for inferences to be made on the basis of the knowledge retrieved. One study[5] allowed the effect of variable names on understanding to be grasped using a paradigm pertinent for studying the inferences made when seeking to understand a program: a completion task. If the statement deleted is 'Count := 0' and the 'counter schema' is recalled thanks to the name of the variable in the update statement 'Count := Count + 1', experts will be able to infer the missing statement more easily than novices. In this study, therefore, it is clear that the name is a semantic index that allows a schema to be activated, which makes it possible to infer the missing part in the schema.

According to this explanatory model of the effect of variable names, we can understand why a performance indicator referring to the outcome of the task cannot measure such an effect. These activation mechanisms are transitory and the processes of comprehension are based on a multiplicity of input data, not merely the meaningful variable names. Thus in Sheppard's experiment, the failure to detect any effect might be due to the fact that the programs were annotated; the effect of the comments might have been to mask, if not to nullify, the effect of the meaningful variable names.

The difficulty of interpreting the absence of an effect, as much as its presence, and the contradictory results observed among the early studies is underlined by Hoc *et al.* (1990). They illustrate it by reference to studies on the effect of various notational structures such as the flowcharts and listings. The results are contradictory: some authors[6] claiming to find a performance improvement with the use of flowcharts, while others[7] found an absence of any effect. We have to wait for later studies to understand which components of the task are affected by the use of flowcharts. Thus Gilmore and Smith (1984) emphasize the fact that the assistance that a given notational structure provides is related to the strategy that the programmers follow to accomplish a task. For a debugging task, the subjects observed followed either a strategy of program execution or a strategy of understanding which allows them to build a mental model of the program. The flowchart, however, is of assistance specifically in the process of execution; the subjects who follow this strategy perform better with the flowcharts than with the listing.

1.1.4 Badly Used Theoretical Borrowings

We have emphasized above the lack of a theoretical framework, which is characteristic of early work. We must recognize, however, that some theoretical ideas were borrowed from psychology but that these ideas were very badly used by computer scientists. The most illuminating example is the borrowing of the notion of short-term memory. A classical distinction in psychology, albeit the subject of a long-standing debate[8], concerns short-term memory, whose capacity is limited, and long-term memory, whose capacity is unlimited. According to a celebrated article (Miller, 1956), the span of short-term memory is restricted to seven items, plus or minus two, which restricts our ability to handle information. This number represents the number of isolated elements (numbers or letters not forming part of a meaningful sequence) that can be kept in short-term memory. This result has been used in computer science to develop complexity metrics. However, a complementary result, just as important, concerns the process of 'chunking'. This process extends the capacity of short-term memory by conceptually regrouping elementary items into items of a different sort. We shall see that, while the concept of short-term memory has been used effectively in the development of program complexity metrics, the equally important concept of chunking has not been taken into account.

Computer science has been interested in developing complexity metrics that allow subjects' performance in programming tasks, especially those that require the understanding of an existing program, to be predicted. Metrics were thus defined that were supposed to allow the comprehensibility of a program to be predicted[9]. McCabe, for example, defined a metric based on the control graph of a program. This metric represents the number of branches in the program.

Halstead took up the idea of a short-term memory span of seven units. He hypothesized that in a given task the items that a programmer would handle correspond to the operators and operands of the programming language. Following on from this, Halstead supposed that the cognitive effort used to understand a program ought to depend on a logarithmic function of the numbers of operands and operators in the program. He thus developed a static complexity metric involving these numbers to predict the comprehensibility of a program.

These metrics have been extensively criticized. As Curtis remarks[10], it is hardly credible to suppose that programmers, with even a little experience, handle information at a level corresponding to items as small as the operators and operands of a program. They must make use of meaningful units corresponding to what is expressed by statements or groups of statements. Through their domain experience, programmers must be able to build larger and larger chunks based on solution patterns. For example, the following might constitute a chunk corresponding to the concept 'calculate the sum of the elements of a table':

```
sum := 0
for i := 1 to n do sum := sum + table(i)
```

An experienced programmer would thus represent this sequence of instructions in the form of a single entity rather than as four unique operators (a total of seven operators) and six unique operands (nine operands in total).

1.1.5 General Criticisms

Finally, we observe that these early studies were severely criticized[11] and that the criticisms gave rise around 1980 to methodological and theoretical debates, which anticipated the theoretical and paradigmatic changes that were to be introduced later.

Hoc emphasizes that most of the studies avoid a psychological analysis of the activity of programming by using a superficial analysis of the task from a purely programming point of view. He condemns the systematic recourse to statistical inference without reference to a scientific psychological theory.

Moher and Schneider criticize the experimental methods, for example, in the choice of subjects (often novices) and the size of the (artificial) programs and tasks used in the experiments. This raises problems over the generality and applicability of the results. One may wonder whether the results obtained with novices in artificial and very constrained situations can be generalized to real situations. They wonder, indeed, whether these studies are, in fact, relevant to real programming. We shall see that the methodological and thematic evolution of later researches allows these obstacles to be overcome.

1.2 Second Period

From a theoretical point of view, the more recent period is characterized by the development of cognitive models of programming and, from a methodological point of view, by a change of paradigm. The use of clinical methods of activity analysis is advocated, alongside with, and as a complement to, strictly experimental methods. The research has two objectives. On the one hand, the theoretical objective is to enrich the theoretical frameworks borrowed from cognitive psychology. This enrichment is expected to come from the analysis of real-world tasks, such analyses being often lacking in experimental psychology. On the other hand, the practical objective is to improve the programming activity by adapting the software tool to its user. This ergonomic objective looks to increase the compatibility between the programmers' representations and the way they handle them, and the features of their working tools.

1.2.1 Theoretical Framework

Later research has been conducted mainly by psychologists and ergonomists or by multidisciplinary teams including psychologists and computer scientists. This research forms part of cognitive psychology. In this field, human activities are modelled in terms of representations and processing. The human being is thus considered as an information processing system[12]. The three most important concepts are representation, processing, and knowledge. Richard states

> What characterizes mental activities is that they construct representations and operate on them. The representations ... are essentially interpretations that consist in using knowledge to attribute an overall meaning to the elements that come out of a perceptual analysis, all this in the context of a situation and a particular task[13].

An important distinction is drawn between representation and knowledge:

> Representations are circumstantial constructions made in a particular context and for specific ends ... The construction of the representation is settled by the task and the decisions to be taken ... Knowledge also consists of constructions but they have a permanence and are not entirely dependent on the task to be carried out; they are stored in long-term memory and, as long as they haven't been changed, they are supposed to maintain the same form[14].

Representation is the cognitive content on which the processing takes place; a new representation is the result of the processing and can thus become the object of further processing. Representations are transitory. In effect, processes are linked to tasks and a new task gives rise to new representations. Some representations can enter the long-term memory, however, and some processes can be stored in the form of procedures.

This research is strongly oriented towards cognitive ergonomics inasmuch as it is concerned with real tasks, professional in the majority of cases. An important distinction is drawn between the concepts of task and activity. The activity is determined by a task. The latter is defined as the set of objective conditions that the subject is capable of taking into account in bringing into action his activity and the cognitive processes that underlie it[15]. It is a question of the objective elements of the situation concerning the end to be reached, the means available for reaching it, and the constraints affecting the deployment of these means. There is a fine distinction[16] to be drawn here between the *prescribed* task in a work situation, which defines what is expected of the subject, and the *effective* task which refers to the representation of the task that he or she constructs. The latter can be defined as the goal and the effective conditions taken into account by the subject.

The tasks that a programmer can carry out on a program already written are varied: detection and correction of errors (debugging), program modification, testing, reuse, documentation. The behaviour employed to reach a defined objective by a particular task is characterized by the activity that is observable and by the cognitive processes that underlie it.

1.2.2 Theoretical Changes

In the psychology of programming we thus pass from a period without theory to a period in which researchers borrow the theoretical frameworks coming out of cognitive psychology. Several pioneering articles thus began to develop such frameworks and also, but to a lesser extent, those from artificial intelligence:

categorization: the approach of Rosch and his colleagues[17] is applied to the categorization of programming problems[18];

understanding of natural language texts: the theory of Kintsch and van Dijk (1978) is applied to the understanding of programs[19];

learning: cognitive and educational models are borrowed to give an account of learning to program[20];

modelling of knowledge: schema theory[21] is borrowed by Soloway and his team[22] to account for the organization of experts' knowledge, and the theory of information processing on knowledge organization in complex domains such as chess[23] is applied to the programming domain[24];

problem solving: Newell and Simon's theory of information processing (1972) is used by Brooks (1977) to take into account the cognitive mechanisms used in program design.

1.2.3 Paradigmatic Changes

As we have already explained, on the methodological plane, there are fewer isolated experimental studies which, while trying to quantify the effect of external factors on programming activity, ignore the cognitive mechanisms responsible for these effects. Recent researches are more of the clinical type, with subtle analyses of the activity according to the paradigm of verbal protocols. This has allowed descriptive models of the activity to be constructed.

This methodological development reflects, in fact, the evolution that has taken place in cognitive psychology during the same period. Alongside the experimental researches, sophisticated methods of observation have been developed, such as the analysis of individual protocols. The validation of hypotheses uses simulation methods at the same time as more refined statistical methods for hypothesis testing[25].

Mental activities can be inferred from behaviour and verbalization and can be simulated by information processing models. In particular, the analysis of verbal and behavioural protocols allows the representations and cognitive processes deployed in an activity to be inferred. Verbalization is an expression of the activity where the subjects' representations and the rules linked to this activity are expressed clearly. Several authors have analysed and criticized the technique of verbalization used in sorting and problem-solving tasks[26].

1.3 Recent Thematic Developments

Research into the psychology of programming has undergone a major change in the last 15 years or so. In 1986 two papers[27], presented at the first workshop on Empirical Studies of Programmers, remarked upon the thematic directions and limitations of the researches carried out up to then in this field: many studies of tasks close to the activity of programming in its strict sense (coding), many studies of programming novices. These remarks raised the question of how far knowledge acquired in this field could be generalized.

The results of the studies were probably dependent on the lack of expertise of the participants, but to what extent? Further, the experimental situations studied, adapted for students, were certainly not representative of real software development situations, in several ways:

- the small size and low complexity of the problems used;
- the straightforward nature of the programming environment used;
- the purely individual character of the activity studied.

To use only novices as subjects did not therefore allow any real ergonomic recommendations for the development of complex programming environments to be made. Another limit to the generalization of the results was that the languages studied were mostly procedural or declarative and that the effect of the programming paradigm on the activity had not been studied.

The recent change addresses these worries through the emergence of research on the following themes:

- the activity of professional programmers and no longer just students;
- the collective and collaborative aspects of software development;
- the activities upstream of coding, e.g. specification and design;
- the effect of languages and programming paradigms on programming activities.

Certain recent researches have been centred on the activity of software experts, especially through the participation of professionals in experimental laboratory studies[28] or field studies[29]. These studies have allowed problems of realistic size to be studied, requiring sometimes several weeks or even several months of development. More generally, they have allowed the modelling and reasoning of experts in a complex field to be addressed.

Studying professional programmers, and not just beginners and students, led to the emergence of another research theme, the learning of new programming languages by experienced programmers. Previously, the learning theme had been restricted to the learning of a first language by programming novices. This new theme allowed the mechanisms of knowledge transfer between languages and even between paradigms to be addressed[30].

For a long time studies of programming centred on activities involving the manipulation of code, for example, code production, debugging, and the understanding of programs. More recently, activities more removed from the production or understanding of code have been studied. These concern the stages before the production of code, such as specification and design. Such research allows us to address the reasoning mechanisms used in solving design problems. Through the study of design, the theme of software reuse has also appeared.

The effect of programming paradigms is a recurrent theme in the literature but it is only very recently that their impact has been faced up to, notably through comparative inter-paradigm studies[31] and through the study of design using an object-oriented programming paradigm and not just a procedural paradigm[32].

Another recent thematic development is to consider programming not simply as an individual activity but also as a collective activity. At the level of a software development team, the themes addressed are the processes of co-operation among designers, the co-ordination processes, and the organizational aspects[33].

These recent studies highlight certain causes of difficulty that programmers experience in carrying out their work. The approach currently followed in developing software, in which, despite the emphasis placed on identifying user needs, there are no real empirical or ergonomic studies of user activity, is partly responsible for these difficulties.

From a practical point of view, research into the psychology of programming poses the problem of the distance between the representations and human processing, on the one hand, and the formal systems allowing these representations themselves to be represented and manipulated at a second level, on the other. From this point of view, the study of programming activities allows us to build models of these activities that can guide the development of programming languages, methods, and problem-solving aids for both expert and novice. This explains its interest for software engineering and will be a constant theme throughout this book.

References

1. See, for example, Curtis, 1982.
2. In particular, Sime, Green and Guest, 1973, 1977
3. Ibid.
4. Gannon, 1976.
5. Soloway and Ehrlich, 1984.
6. Wright, 1977.
7. Shneidermann, Mayer, McKay and Heller, 1977.
8. Florès, 1970.
9. Halstead, 1977; McCabe, 1976; Schroeder, 1983; Sunohara, Takano, Uehara and Ohkawa, 1981.
10. Curtis, 1980; Curtis, Forman, Brooks, Soloway and Ehrlich, 1984.
11. Brooks, 1980; Curtis, 1984; Hoc, 1982a; 1982b; Laughery and Lauchery, 1985; Moher and Schneider, 1982; Sheil, 1981.
12. Newell and Simon, 1972.
13. Richard, 1990, p. 9.
14. Ibid. p. 10.
15. Leplat and Pailhous, 1977.
16. Leplat and Hoc, 1983.
17. Rosch, Mervis, Gray, Johnson and Boyes-Braem, 1976; Rosch, 1978.
18. Adelson, 1981.
19. Atwood and Ramsey, 1978.
20. Mayer, 1981.
21. Schank and Abelson, 1977.
22. Soloway and Ehrlich, 1984.
23. Chase and Simon, 1973.

24. McKeithen, Reitman, Reuter and Hirtle, 1981.
25. Richard, Bonnet & Ghiglione, 1990.
26. Ericsson and Simon, 1980; Hoc, 1984a; Hoc and Leplat, 1983.
27. Curtis, 1986; Soloway, 1986.
28. See, for example, Détienne, 1990a.
29. See, for example, Visser, 1987.
30. Chatel, Détienne and Borne, 1992; Scholtz and Wiedenbeck, 1990a, 1990b; Wu and Anderson, 1991.
31. See, for example, Lee and Pennington, 1994; Petre, 1990.
32. See, for example, Détienne and Rist, 1995.
33. Bürkle, Gryczan and Züllighoven, 1995; Curtis and Walz, 1990; D'Astous, Détienne, Robillard and Visser, 1997, 1998; Herbsleb, Klein, Olson, Brunner, Olson and Harding, 1995; Krasner, Curtis and Iscoe, 1987; Robillard, D'Astous, Détienne and Visser, 1998.

2. What Is a Computer Program?

What is a computer program? In Section 2.1 we shall try to clarify this point with definitions from a computing point of view and from a psychological point of view. We shall draw a parallel between research on the handling (production and comprehension) of natural language text and the handling of program text. From this point of view, two questions seem particularly relevant. First, is it possible to bring together theoretically a computer program and a natural language text. What type of text – narrative or procedural? Second, what are the differences between programming languages and natural languages? These questions will be addressed in Sections 2.2 and 2.3. These discussions will allow us to consider a wider definition of computer programs in Section 2.4.

2.1 Definition of a Program

2.1.1 From a Computer Point of View

Syntactically, a program is a text constructed according to a well-defined set of grammatical rules. Semantically, a program expresses a calculation or, to be more precise, a set of calculations. Thus, according to Pair (1990), to program is to transform specifications that describe a function into a program, that is, a text that can be interpreted by a machine in order to calculate that function.

A computer program is the expression, in a certain language, of a calculation or procedure – but also the expression of certain objects. This distinguishes two aspects of programming: the decomposition of a calculation in order to produce an algorithm and the definition of objects. According to Wirth (1976), it is the combination of these two aspects, the algorithm and the data structures (more generally, the objects) that make up a program.

In imperative programming, whatever the programming language, three control constructions lie at the base of the calculations: iteration, sequence and selection. The concept of a variable is equally applicable to any type of program written in an imperative programming language. The structure of the data to be manipulated may be defined explicitly or not, according to the language. The concept of object is peculiar to object-oriented programming.

2.1.2 From a Psychological Point of View

From this point of view, we need to distinguish between the surface structure of a program, its deep structure[a], and its execution by the machine.

The surface structure of a program corresponds to its textual structure, in other words, the surface units, explicit in the program, and the way in which they are arranged. The deep structure corresponds to the representation of relations that are not explicit in the surface structure. This distinction will be investigated increasingly deeply as the book continues, especially in the light of models for the production and understanding of texts. It is based on the different types of relation and levels of abstraction that one can construct starting from a program[1]. We can identify, for example, the linear structure, the flow of control, the data flow, the plans, and the hierarchical organization of goals and sub-goals. We shall illustrate these different types of relation with reference to the program for calculating an average shown in Fig. 2.1.

The linear structure of the program is well represented by its textual version. The flow of control represents the order in which the instructions are executed, an ordering controlled by the three control constructs: iteration, sequence and

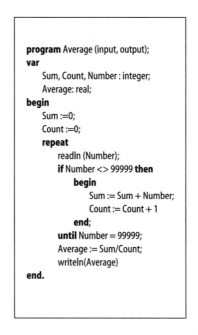

```
program Average (input, output);
var
        Sum, Count, Number : integer;
        Average: real;
begin
        Sum :=0;
        Count :=0;
        repeat
            readln (Number);
            if Number <> 99999 then
                begin
                    Sum := Sum + Number;
                    Count := Count + 1
                end;
            until Number = 99999;
            Average := Sum/Count;
            writeln(Average)
end.
```

Fig. 2.1 Pascal program to calculate the average of a set of numbers.

---

[a]The concepts of surface structure and deep structure were introduced first in linguistics by Noam Chomsky (1965). They were initially seen as a powerful technique for linguistic description, which could be used to explain, for example, the relationship between the two sentences *A dog bit me* and *I was bitten by a dog*. Chomsky went on to make much stronger claims concerning the idea of deep structure. Readers who are familiar with the concepts in linguistics are warned that the usage of the terms here, while obviously related to the linguistic usage, is significantly different from it.

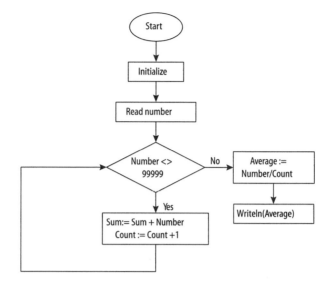

Fig. 2.2 Flow of control in a program to calculate an average.

selection. Figure 2.2 shows the control structure of the program as a flow chart; we could equally well have represented it as a Jackson structure chart.

The data flow view of the program shows the data and their transformation in the course of the processing; this is shown in Fig. 2.3.

Finally, a program allows at least one main goal to be achieved but this goal may be made up from several sub-goals. Figure 2.4 shows this decomposition into goals and sub-goals[b]. With each sub-goal that is a terminal node of the tree a plan is associated, that is, a set of actions that, when carried out in the appropriate order, allows the sub-goal to be achieved. A program can therefore be represented as a combination of plans, each plan been made up of a sequence of actions allowing a goal to be achieved[2]. Figure 2.5 shows to which plan each of the instructions in the program belongs.

Anticipating later chapters, we can distinguish between surface structure and deep structure on the basis of these different types of relation. Thus the surface items[c] correspond to the elementary operations and their linear structure, as well as to the items defined by the control structure and their organization. The deep structure includes the data flows, the objects (in object-oriented programming), and the hierarchical organization of goals and plans. Hence, any representation of a program is essentially multi-dimensional.

---

[b]This hierarchical representation can be refined by introducing objects. One can then present objects either as central, with goals and sub-goals organized around them, or as secondary and associated with sub-goals and plans.
[c]This is true for languages of a procedural nature but not necessarily true for non-procedural languages.

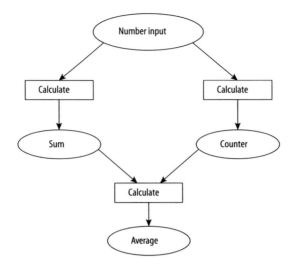

Fig. 2.3 Data flow in a program to calculate the average.

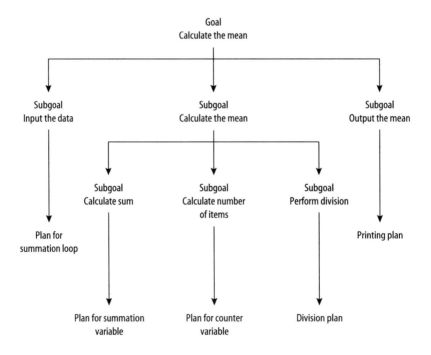

Fig. 2.4 Hierarchical representation of goals and plans.

Execution by the Machine

A programming language is a code in the semiotic sense of the term[3], that is a system of two-sided symbols, one side being the form and the other the content or meaning (syntax and semantics in computing terminology). Learning a programming language consists, therefore, in acquiring not only the syntax of the language but also the rules of operation of the virtual machine underlying it.

For the machine, a program statement represents a procedure, not just a static concept[4]. Each instruction can be described as a set of transactions for the machine that will execute it. For example, an instruction of the form

<variable-name> ::= <constant>

(e.g. X:= 4) might give rise to the following sequence of operations:

1. find where in memory the constant (e.g. 4) is stored;
2. copy the value of the constant to a temporary location;
3. find where in memory the value of the variable (e.g. A) is to be stored;
4. copy the value in the temporary location into the location assigned to A;
5. proceed to the next statement.

The detail of such a sequence depends, of course, on the design of the machine that has to execute the program and on the design of the compiler that translates it. Further, the execution of the program can be represented at multiple levels. Each of the above operations may itself consist of a sequence of lower level operations.

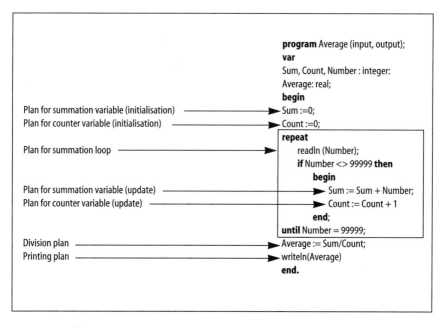

Fig. 2.5 Representation of the combination of plans in the program code.

2.2 Program vs Text

A computer program is the expression of a procedure and data structures in a certain language. Insofar as the expression is in a certain language, a program can be considered a text. Research on the understanding of computer programs has been strongly influenced by this working hypothesis. The models considered in accounting for the understanding of programs have thus largely been borrowed from research into the understanding of natural language text. We shall examine the parallels between, on the one hand, computer programs and narrative texts, and, on the other hand, computer programs and procedural text.

2.2.1 A Program Seen as a Narrative Text

Numerous authors have drawn a parallel between programs and narrative texts, that is, stories. As for narrative texts, one can represent the deep structure of a program as a hierarchy of goals and of plans allowing these goals to be achieved. One difference, emphasized by Black, Kay and Solway (1986), is that the plans are very much mixed together in a program, something that is rare in narrative texts. This could be one of the reasons why understanding programs is difficult. This difference disappears, however, if we look at the parallel with a particular type of narrative text, namely murder mysteries[5]. In such stories, the reader has similarly to construct the goals and plans of the protagonists, starting from the information dispersed through the surface structure of the text.

2.2.2 A Program Seen as a Procedural Text

Any representation of the deep structure of programs or of procedural texts is multi-dimensional. We can identify a hierarchy of goals and plans (as for a narrative text) but also causal and temporal relations between states, actions and events[6]. In programs, the relations can involve communication between variables (data flows) and communication between objects (client-server relationships in object-oriented programming).

A comparison between programs and instruction manuals shows that understanding programs, like understanding manuals, uses processes for constructing procedural rules. An instruction manual typically provides general information on the use of a system rather than specific procedures to be used in specific situations. The reader does not build up a representation of the text but a set of rules that can be applied in situations as yet unspecified. As Robertson and Yu (1990) remark:

> Similarly, a programmer seeking to understand a program that routes telephone calls is looking for the expression of a method, a set of rules that will work in many situations. He or she is not trying to find a particular routing solution.

2.3 Programming Languages vs Natural Languages

2.3.1 Unambiguous Nature of Programming Languages

There is one essential difference between programming languages and natural languages, namely that the former are syntactically unambiguous. The syntactic rules of a programming language must satisfy a set of very strict constraints, which prevent any possibility of a program written in the language from exhibiting the lexical and syntactic ambiguities that occur in any natural language[d]. Thus, if one tries to express the structure of the programming language as a set of propositions, this is strongly constrained if not, indeed, reduced to the syntactic rules of the language[7].

Natural language text uses anaphora, that is, indirect reference through pronouns or pronominal adjectives. (For example, 'The printer is connected to the parallel port. *It* has only a limited range of fonts.') This is, indeed, an important research theme in psycholinguistics. In contrast, anaphora is rare in programming languages[e]. It is interesting to note that something similar is true of procedural text, in which nouns are often repeated rather than replaced by a pronoun in contexts where they would be replaced in narrative texts[8].

2.3.2 Use of Natural Language or Pseudo-Code

Certain nominal elements are not constrained by the programming language or, more precisely, are constrained only trivially; these are the names that the programmer gives to items in the program, such as variables, constants, routines (procedures and functions), classes, etc. These names are, in general, lexical elements of a natural language, even if they are sometimes constrained by syntactic rules that cause them to be abbreviated. Such terms have no meaning for the computer, except to identify the item, but they have meaning for the programmer. Further, as we shall see in Chapter 5, they are very important in the understanding process. But they can present ambiguities in the same way as in a natural language.

Software documentation may be written in natural language or in pseudo-code, i.e. a language intermediate between formal language and natural language. Designers produce a great deal of information when they design programs – design notes, provisional descriptions or the descriptions and explanations that document the final program[9]. Thus, even if the final goal of the design activity is to produce a list of instructions in a programming language, information expressed in natural language makes up an integral part of the designer's solution[10].

2.4 Toward a Broader Definition

What has been said so far allows us to consider a wider definition of computer programs. On the one hand, at the level of deep structure, this should emphasize

---

[d]There may, of course, be semantic ambiguity due, for example, to real-time effects.
[e]The history operators in the UNIX C-shell are probably the best known examples of anaphoric reference in programming languages.

the complex, multi-dimensional character of the representation constructed. A program can therefore be represented as a tree of goals and sub-goals, with objects represented as central or secondary entities, and plans for attaining the goals. Different types of relations, such as data flows, communication between objects, the structure of plans, can be represented.

On the other hand, this definition does not restrict programming simply to the production and expression of a procedure in a programming language. Due to the special use for which computer programs are intended, execution by a machine and use (producing or reading) by a human, the final product includes at the same time instructions in the programming language and in natural language. We therefore consider that, at the level of its surface structure, a program is a 'text' written in a programming language and in natural language. We shall see in this book that the information expressed in each of these two types of language has its own role to play in design and understanding.

References

1. Kant and Newell, 1985; Pennington, 1987a; Pennington and Grabowski, 1990.
2. Rist, 1991.
3. Hoc, 1987a.
4. Mayer, 1987.
5. Robertson and Yu, 1990.
6. Baudet and Cordier, 1995.
7. Robertson, 1990.
8. Puglielli, 1990.
9. Bellamy, 1994a; Davies, 1996; Henry, Green, Gilmore and Davies, 1992.
10. Détienne, Rouet, Burkhardt and Deleuze-Dordron, 1996.

3. *Software Design: Theoretical Approaches*

A special feature of software design is that the problems to be solved are 'ill-defined'. There is also a distinction to be drawn between the problems of producing programs and the problems of producing results. We shall discuss these characteristics in Section 3.1. We then go on to present three theoretical approaches used in studying the activity of software design: the knowledge-centred approach, the strategy-centred approach and the organization-centred approach.

The knowledge-centred approach, discussed in Section 3.2, involves identifying and formalizing the knowledge of the expert within the framework of the theory of schemas. According to this approach, the activity of designing a program consists, in part, of activating schemas kept in memory that are suitable for handling certain problems, and of combining them to construct a program. This work concentrates on analysing the knowledge of experts and pays little attention to the way the knowledge is used. Thus it largely ignores the strategic aspect of program design.

The strategy-centred approach is discussed in Section 3.3. It seems that the expert is characterized, not only by more abstract knowledge, organized hierarchically, but also by a wider and more adaptable range of strategies than the novice. Design strategies can be described in terms of several different features, for example, whether they are top-down or bottom-up. An important research question is to specify the condition for adopting particular strategies. Externally the choice is determined by the characteristics of the notation, the features of the environment, and the problem type. The internal determinants are linked to the subject's expertise in computing, especially the availability in his or her memory of programming schemas. But it is often the interaction between several factors that determines the strategy.

Section 3.4 is concerned with the approach which is centred on the organization of the design activity, a more 'meta' level than the strategy-centred approach. Two types of model contrast with each other:

1. The hierarchical model based on normative models inspired by programming methods.

2. Opportunistic models, based on the results of empirical studies, which emphasize how the real activity deviates from a strictly hierarchical model.

Finally, some studies place the accent on the iterative character of the design activity, drawing a parallel with models of text production. We shall also look at the note-taking mechanisms that are used in design, demonstrating that documentation is an inherent part of the design process.

What distinguishes an expert from a novice? What are the formative stages of the expertise? Can we identify several different types of expertise? These questions will be discussed in Section 3.5.

Studies of program design have practical implications, especially for the ergonomic specifications of programming environments best adapted to their users. This is the topic of Section 3.6, while the final section explores the limits of existing work and the prospects for the future.

■ ■

3.1 Features of the Problems of Program Design

3.1.1 Ill-defined Problems

Program design has been mainly studied within the framework of research into problem-solving activities. The problem-solving activity is usually described as being made up of three successive phases; understanding the problem, research and development of the solution, and coding the solutions. In fact, these phases are not purely sequential because there is interaction between them.

Program design, like other design activities (architectural design, for example) has the special characteristic of being ill defined, in the sense that some of the specifications of the problem are missing and part of solving the problem is to introduce new constraints. Another feature is that there exist several acceptable solutions for the same problem, which cannot be evaluated according to any single criterion.

An equally important aspect of the program design activity is that designers use knowledge from at least two domains, the application (or problem) domain and the computing domain, between which they establish a mapping. Simplifying, we can say that programmers construct at least two types of mental model; a model of the problem and its solution in terms of the application domain and a model in computing terms. Part of their work consists of passing from one model to the other. Depending on the features of the design situation, the distance between these models will be bigger or smaller. One might hypothesize that some programming paradigms, for example, object-orientation, reduce this distance for particular application domains.

3.1.2 Problems of Program Production

In general, solving a problem is the same thing as working out a solution. However, two different types of problem-solving situation[1] can be distinguished according to what type of solution is produced, either a procedure for obtaining a result or the result itself:

1. In a result-producing situation, the subject concentrates on the goal assigned and, if a procedure is developed, this is only secondary. It will usually be stored in memory in executable form. The subject has not therefore constructed a representation of this procedure.

2. When a program has to be produced, the subject concentrates on working out a procedure. This means constructing a representation of the structure of the procedure over and above the result required.

The distinction between the two situations is well illustrated by the task of sorting a set of names into alphabetical order. Most literate people can produce the required result with little difficulty. It is much harder, however, to describe a procedure for carrying out this task in general.

Clearly, designing a program is much more like the second kind of task. It consists, indeed, in constructing a representation of a procedure and, further, of expressing this procedure in a certain design notation or language.

3.2 Knowledge-centred Approaches

As we shall see, identifying and formalizing the knowledge of expert programmers has given rise to a great deal of research.

3.2.1 Theory of Schemas

Researchers in program design are generally agreed that there are three types of knowledge that serve to distinguish experts from novices:

1. Syntactic knowledge, which defines the syntactic and lexical elements of a programming language, for example, the fact that, in C, the **if** statement takes the form **if** (*condition*) *statement*.

2. Semantic knowledge, which refers to the concepts, such as the notion of a variable, that make it possible to understand what happens when a line of code is executed.

3. Schematic knowledge, that is, programming schemas that represent generic solutions.

The theory of schemas has been widely used to describe the knowledge of expert programmers[2]. It is a theory of the organization of knowledge in memory and of the processes for making use of this knowledge. A schema is a data structure which represents generic concepts stored in memory[a]. The notion of a schema was developed in artificial intelligence and in psychological studies of text understanding.

Before going further into schemas we must make a distinction between the idea of a schema and the idea of a solution plan. A schema is a knowledge structure. A solution plan is a sequence of actions in a program which will achieve the goal of the program. (This idea is illustrated in Fig. 2.3 of Chapter 2.) For the expert, a plan often represents a special case or an instance of a programming schema. A schema being a structure of variables to which is associated a set of possible values, the special case is characterized by a combination of specific values chosen to achieve a specific goal in a specific program.

---

[a]The concept of a *frame* is widely used in artificial intelligence and there seems to be no consistent difference in usage between the terms *frame* and *schema*.

3.2.2 Programming Schemas

Studies of programming show that expert programmers keep in their memory schemas specific to the programming domain. We can classify such schemas into the following two types:

- Elementary programming schemas representing knowledge about control structures and variables (called 'control plans' and 'variable plans' by Soloway). For example, a counter variable schema can be formalized as following:
    - Goal: count the occurrences of an action
    - Initialization: count:= n
    - Update: count:=count+increment
    - Type: integer
    - Context: loop

  Schemas of this sort can be thought of as consisting of a frame and slots, as this example illustrates. Prototypical values are zero for the initialization and one for the increment. Plans which are instances of elementary programming schema are also illustrated in Fig. 2.5 of Chapter 2;

- algorithmic schemas or complex programming schemas represent knowledge about structure of algorithms. For example, some programmers will be familiar with a variety of algorithms for sorting and searching. These algorithms are more or less abstract and more or less independent of the programming language, and they can be described as made up of elementary schemas. For example, a sequential search schema is less abstract than a search schema and can be described as being composed, in part, of an counter variable schema.

Another way of classifying programming schemas is according to their degree of dependence on the programming language[3]:

- tactical and strategic schemas, which are independent of the programming language (or, at least, within a single programming paradigm);
- implementation schemas, which are dependent on a particular programming language.

More strictly, we should refer to dependence on particular features of programming languages. Implementation schemas for operating on trees may be dependent on the possibility of recursion in the programming language; many but by no means all languages support this.

Schemas are related to each other in various ways:

- composition, that is, a schema is made up of several simpler schemas;
- specialization, i.e. the 'is a' relationship. A sequential search schema 'is a' search schema and a counter-controlled running total loop schema 'is a' running total loop plan;
- implementation, i.e., an implementation schema in a specific programming language implements a more abstract tactical or strategic schema that is language independent. Thus a for-loop schema in C or Pascal is an implementation of an abstract counter-controlled running total loop schema;

Rist (1986) introduced the notion of the 'focus' or 'focal line' of a schema. The focus is the part of the schema that directly implements its goal. Thus, for the counter schema, the focus would be the incrementing of the counter. The focus is the most important part of the schema. Certainly it is the part that is most available when a schema is retrieved. In design, the focus is the part that is recovered and expressed first, the code being constructed around it.

3.2.3 Other Types of Schema

Programming schemas, which are rich in knowledge and content, can be contrasted with structural schemas. In studies of the production and understanding of text, especially those using the story grammar approach, the structural schemas are often called the superstructure. A text of a certain type (e.g. a scientific article) can be described by a structure specific to that type of text. The knowledge of this structure, remembered in the form of the superstructure, can thus guide the production and understanding of this type of text.

The notion of role, introduced by Rist (1986) in the programming field, can be considered similar to this notion of structural schema. For example, a structural schema for a functional program is composed of three roles: input, calculate and output. A structural schema for classes of object-oriented programs is composed of the following roles: creation, initialization, reading access, writing access, input and output.

Programmers' ability to write or understand programs depends also on their familiarity with structural schemas.

Domain specific schemas, like programming schemas, are rich in knowledge and content. Détienne (1986) suggests that, as they become familiar with a problem domain, experts develop domain-specific schemas, that is, knowledge schemas representing their knowledge of certain types of problem. Thus an expert in invoicing and sales ledger applications will have a schema for discount structures.

3.2.4 Rules of Discourse

Experts also have rules of discourse that control the construction of programs and especially the instantiation of schemas during design. When designing a program, experts retrieve suitable programming schemas from memory and instantiate them according to the particular problem they are solving. This instantiation is controlled by the rules of discourse. Three typical examples[4] are:

- the name of a variable must reflect its function;
- if a condition is tested, the condition must have the potential of being true;
- do not use the same piece of code for two different purposes in a non-obvious way.

In professional software engineering organizations, the rules of discourse are usually formalized in sets of coding standards for the different programming languages that the organization uses. Checking programs to ensure that they comply with these standards is a normal part of the quality assurance procedures.

3.2.5 Limitations of Schemas

The theory of schemas allows us to take into account certain cognitive mechanisms used not only in programming design but also in learning programming and in understanding a program. Program design consists, in part, of activating schemas held in memory, suitable for handling certain problems, and in combining them to build a program. Learning to program is characterized by the progressive construction of programming schemas. Understanding a program consists, in part, of activating schemas stored in memory using indexes extracted from the program code and then inferring certain information starting from the schemas retrieved (cf. Section 6.3.1). This approach in terms of schemas is limited because it takes little account of other processes that are found in these activities, which are bottom-up and more constructive.

3.3 Strategy-centred Approach

All the work described above is centred on the analysis of the knowledge of experts rather than on analysis of the way this knowledge is put to use. In other words, it does not address the strategic aspect of program design. As we have already remarked, it seems that, in comparison to the novice, the expert is characterized not only by more abstract, hierarchically organized knowledge but also by a broader range of more versatile strategies. Thus experts choose their design strategies on the basis of factors such as the familiarity of the situation, the characteristics of the application task, and the notational features of the language. Novices often experience difficulty not only because of the lack of adequate knowledge but also because of the lack of suitable strategies for responding to a specific situation; thus, in some cases, they may have the necessary knowledge but be incapable of accessing it or using it.

3.3.1 Classification of Strategies

Design strategies can be classified along several axes[5]: top-down vs bottom-up, forward vs backward development, breadth-first vs depth-first, procedural vs declarative.

Top-down vs Bottom-up

A solution may be developed either top-down or bottom-up, that is from the more abstract to the less abstract or vice versa. In the first case the programmer develops the solution at an abstract level and then refines it, progressively adding more and more detail. In the second case, the solution is developed at a very detailed level before its more abstract structure is identified. Top-down development is usually associated with experts while novices typically try to develop bottom-up, by writing directly in the final programming language and then building the abstract structure of the solution. Nevertheless, bottom-up development is used by experts, particularly when libraries of reusable components are available (see Chapter 4) or when a product line is being developed[6].

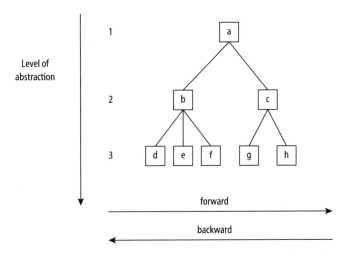

Fig. 3.1 Working out a solution along two axes: abstraction and forward/backward.

Forward vs Backward Development

A design strategy is described as forward development when the solution is developed in direction of execution of the procedure. It is described as backward if it is developed in the direction opposite to that of the execution of the procedure. The use of a forward strategy by beginners often reflects the mental execution of the solution: they rely on this mental execution to work out the solution[7]. In such cases, the development of the solution relies not on computing knowledge but on knowledge of the problem domain: beginners recall known procedures that they develop in a forward sense. Experts also use forward development when they retrieve a known solution schema from memory and implement the elements of the schema in the order in which they will be executed[8]. The direction of development may be backward when no known schema or procedure is available. In Fig. 3.1, a forward strategy would consist in developing level 2 in the order b-c and level 3 in the order d-e-f-g-h.

Breadth-first vs Depth-first

A breadth-first strategy means developing all the elements of the solution at one level of abstraction before proceeding to the next, more detailed, level of abstraction. A depth-first strategy means that one element of the system is developed to all levels of abstraction before any other element is developed. In Fig. 3.1, breadth-first development would mean first developing everything at level 2 (b-c or c-b) and then everything at level 3 (d-e-f-g-h in any order). Depth-first development would mean a-b-d then, e, then f, then a-c-g, then h.

On this axis, it is worth noting that we may distinguish between exploratory activities and development activities. Exploratory activity consists in generating and evaluating alternative solutions in a search space that can also be described at several levels of abstraction. The exploration itself can also be done breadth-first or depth-first.

Wirth's stepwise refinement strategy[9] can be characterized as top-down, breadth-first. The problem is broken down into sub-problems and, at a given level of abstraction, the solution is explored and developed completely[10]. The term 'balanced development' has been used to describe this situation, when the solution is developed completely at level n, then at level $n + 1$, and so on until the least abstract level, that of code, is reached. Experts are observed to use such a strategy to solve problems that are relatively simple and familiar.

Procedural vs Declarative

The development of a solution is said to be procedural when it is the structure of the procedure that controls the solution; the solution is then based on aims or procedures. The development is said to be declarative when static properties, such as objects and roles, control the solution.

This distinction is similar to, but more general than, the distinction between procedure-driven and data-driven software development methods. Methods that concentrate on data analysis and database design would thus be described as declarative, while methods that emphasize functional decomposition would be described as functional.

Mental Simulation

A number of other strategies have been described, notably mental simulation. Simulation can be used to evaluate a solution. In fact, designers often use mental simulation on a partial or complete solution at a higher or lower level of abstraction or on passages of code that they are seeking to understand. Simulation provides a way of verifying that a solution meets the desired objectives and a way of integrating partial solutions by controlling their interactions.

3.3.2 Triggering Conditions

As we have said, it is important to investigate the circumstances under which particular strategies are triggered.

Cognitive Dimensions

Psychologists have studied the notational structure of programming languages and the features of programming environments by identifying different characteristics, called cognitive dimensions[11], that have an effect on the programming activity. Several such dimensions have been identified, among them the following:

hidden dependencies: these arise when a relationship between different items of information is explicit in one direction but not the other. The infamous 'goto' statement is an example of a hidden dependency. It is easily possible to follow this in a forward direction, that is, in the order of execution, but not in the backward direction. This makes some information difficult to find, for example, the conditions under which particular statements are executed;

consistency: this is the property of syntactic and lexical uniformity. For example, the syntax of an integer expression, whether it is a value to be assigned or an array subscript, should always be the same; this was not always the case in early programming languages, such as FORTRAN 2. Consistency makes learning a language or an environment easier;

premature commitment: this occurs when programmers are obliged to take certain decisions before they have all the information necessary. Ordering constraints in some programming environments oblige the programmer to define certain items first, for example, it may be necessary to define a class before using it in the program;

redundancy: this feature may make a program easier to understand but it may make coding longer and more difficult;

resistance to change ('viscosity'): this refers to the amount of effort necessary to make a modification. Thus, a modification at one place may oblige the programmer to make other changes. For example, in Pascal, the need to introduce an extra variable to store a temporary result will lead to the need to add a declaration of the variable in the declaration Section of the code. In general, the more redundant the notation, the more resistant programs are to change;

progressive evaluation: can a partly completed program be tested or evaluated in some other way? Clearly this property helps with reviewing design and code;

'role expressiveness': can the reader easily see what is the relationship between each component of the program and the whole?

visibility: is each part of the program simultaneously visible? Or is it possible at least to display two parts of the program side by side?

The first five of these are primarily programming language issues while the last three are environment issues; however, there is significant interaction between the language and the environment so that, for example, an environment can alleviate the resistance to change evinced by a programming language, by showing the programmer where consequential changes need to be made.

The Notational Structure of Programming Languages

Cognitive dimensions allow us to characterize certain aspects of the notational structure of programming languages. Studies have shown that these dimensions have an effect on the design strategies that the designers follow; there is some evidence to suggest that the effect is greater for designers with an intermediate level of experience than for either experts or beginners[12].

Consider the case of Pascal and Basic. Pascal is much more resistant to change than Basic, because a change in one place is likely to require many other modifications to the code. This is due, *inter alia*, to Pascal's high level of redundancy; every variable must be declared, for example, which is not the case in Basic.

An empirical study[13] has shown that if the notation exhibits strong resistance to change (Pascal in comparison to Basic), the designer tries to minimize the modifications to be made to the code during the design and coding. The Pascal programmer thus uses a top-down strategy based on successive refinement, with frequent taking of notes. The Basic programmer adopts a much more linear and progressive strategy, which leads to frequent backtracking when additions or modifications are to be made.

It may not, however, be the characteristics of the programming language that lead to this difference. Pascal programmers will probably have been taught the language in an academic environment, in which successive refinement is advocated as the 'correct' approach to program design; furthermore most text books on Pascal take this approach. Basic programmers are much more likely to be self taught and thus to adopt a less sophisticated approach; Basic text books are much less likely to advocate successive refinement.

Features of Programming Environments

Cognitive dimensions have also been used to characterize programming environments. Again, studies have shown that the cognitive dimensions of the programming environment affect the strategies adopted by designers. One such study[14] evaluated the object-oriented CO2 language and its environment. This environment has strict ordering constraints, which lead to premature commitment. For example, it is necessary to declare a class before being able to refer to it in a method. This feature of the environment very clearly requires a top-down design strategy since the designers define the classes at an abstract level before developing the code of the methods and using the classes. The study also showed that such a strategy, enforced by the features of the environment, was the cause of errors and that much backtracking was then necessary to modify the erroneous or incomplete class model.

There is a clear conflict here between generally accepted software engineering principles, which emphasize the importance of the top-down approach and declaration before use in producing quality software, and the ease with which small programs can be written and understood.

Problem Type

The type of problem also affects the choice of strategy[15]. A problem can be forward or backward, procedural or declarative, just as a strategy can be. A declarative problem is characterized by a strong data structure (whether of input or output data) data. The program structure is strongly linked to the structure of the data, which provides reliable guidance in the search for a solution. In such a case, the designer will adopt a declarative strategy. If it is the structure of the input data that is strong, the strategy will be declarative and forward. If it is the structure of the results that is strong, the strategy will be declarative and retrospective.

A procedural problem is characterized by a complex procedural structure. The structure of the data gives little help in solving such problems and it is the procedural structure that will guide the design activity. The designer will thus adopt a procedural strategy.

This classification has recently been refined within the framework of object-oriented design[16]. In this paradigm, the declarative/procedural classification does not appear sufficient. A new dimension has been identified: this characterizes not only the structure of the data (or objects in OO) and the structure of the procedure, but also the way in which the two are associated. The strategy adopted by experts is declarative when the problem exhibits a hierarchical solution structure with vertical communication between the objects, while the strategy is procedural when the problem exhibits a flat solution structure with horizontal communications between the objects. In the first case, the procedural structure can be fairly easily deduced from the object structure, which is not true in the second case.

The relationship between the problem and the strategy illuminates, and is illuminated by, a consideration of structured development methods. The use of the structure of the input data to guide the structure of the program is a fundamental idea that goes back to Jackson Structured Programming[17]. The distinction between problem types also explains why the search for a universal development method is doomed to failure.

Internal Factors

Some internal determinants are linked to the computing expertise of the subject and to the programming schemas constructed in his or her memory[18]. Thus experts can follow a top-down, forward strategy for problems that are familiar to them and for which they already have a schema, while the novice will rather follow a bottom-up, retrospective strategy. Empirical studies[19] show that experts use the strategy of successive refinement, i.e. top-down, breadth-first, for familiar problems of reasonable size.

3.4 Organization-centred Approach

For studying the organization of the design activity, two contrasting types of model can be used: the hierarchical model, based on normative models inspired by programming methods, and opportunistic models, based on the results of empirical studies, which emphasize how real activity deviates from a strictly hierarchical model.[b]

3.4.1 Hierarchical Models

The hierarchical model has been strongly influenced by structured programming. According to this model[20], the process of breaking down a problem into a solution is essentially top-down and a breadth-first search for a solution is preferred. All the goals (or functions) of the solution are identified at a certain level of abstraction before being refined successively to more and more detailed levels. This refinement consists either in detailing the abstract elements of the solution or in choosing to deploy more general functions. The prescribed process consists in working at one level of abstraction at a time, preferring to develop the solution breadth-first rather than depth-first.

3.4.2 Opportunistic Models

These models take account of observed deviations from the hierarchical plan and of the conditions that trigger such deviations[21]. While designers seem to accept

---

[b]Although this contrast between hierarchical design and opportunistic design is challenged by some authors, the importance of opportunistic deviations in professional activity can certainly not be called into question.

the hierarchical model as the paradigm for what they are doing, frequently because this is how they have been taught, they often behave very differently. Real design is organized opportunistically: a bottom-up approach is used as often as a top-down, and depth-first searching may be used in preference to breadth-first, depending on the situation. Thus the hierarchical structure reflects the result of the activity but not the organization of the activity itself.

The studies cited bear witness, on the one hand, to the focusing on different aspects of the solution or on different sub-problems that takes place in the course of the design activity, and, on the other hand, to the possible use of different design strategies to handle different aspects of the process. A solution of hierarchical type is developed by jumping between different levels of abstraction. For example, designers sometimes give priority to refining certain aspects of the solution that they deem critical[22]. This is particularly useful for detecting potential interactions with other parts of the solution.

The adoption of an opportunistic strategy can be triggered by several different factors such as resource limitations or a process of 'meta-cognitive management'.

The plan that guides the design process is hierarchical and opportunistic episodes can be triggered by failures of working memory[23]; information about the hierarchical plan and the way it is being followed is lost when the capacity of the working memory is exceeded. This effect has been demonstrated by asking subjects simultaneously to design and describe orally what they are doing; this double task overloads the working memory, which produces opportunistic deviations in the design process.

Opportunistic deviations are controlled at a meta-cognitive level by criteria that allow the cost of alternative actions to be calculated[24]. One of the reasons that lead the designer to deviate from a hierarchical plan may be the economic utilization of the resources available. If information needed to handle one aspect of the solution is not available, the subject puts it to one side. On the other hand the economic utilization of the information available can lead to certain aspects of the solution at different levels of detail being treated prematurely in comparison with the ideal hierarchical plan of the process. The real process of design will thus be out of phase with the ideal model, either lagging or leading it. Notes made by designers during the process often testify to these phenomena.

3.4.3 The Iterative Nature of Design

Another characteristic of the program design activity is its iterative nature, involving cycles of designing, coding and revising. The cycles are generally accompanied by intensive note-taking.

While the approaches presented above put the emphasis on the parallel with problem solving models, another interesting parallel is with the production of natural language texts. The model of Hayes and Flower[25], one of the most influential cognitive models of text production, identifies three phases in the process of drafting a text:

- planning the structure of the text: the organization of the ideas is a function of domain knowledge and the setting of goals depends on the communication objectives;

- translating the plan of the text into a linguistic representation;
- reviewing the text.

An important feature of this model is that the global process is iterative rather than strictly linear. Further, the ordering of the phases is not strictly predefined[c]. In effect, the organization of the phases depends on the writer's strategy. One effect of the non-linear character is that the writer generates many intermediate results, planning notes, temporary text, additions, etc. The writer also revises versions of the text in such a way as to improve its clarity, its coherence and/or to make the development of the ideas more convincing[26]. Even if the first version of the text is, in general, comprehensible, the revised version accords better with the writer's objectives.

Program design also includes planning, translation and reviewing phases (usually called problem solving or analysis, coding or implementation, and review). Planning demands both the retrieval of knowledge relevant to the solution of the problem and the construction of an abstract solution. The process of translation is equivalent to the implementation of a solution in a specific programming language. Finally, the review process can involve revising the implementation, the abstract solution or the problem representation. It has been shown that cycles including these three phases are produced in the course of software development[27]. The review process leads to changes that may be stylistic, strategic or tactical. Stylistic changes involve changes only to the coding, often to make the program comply with the standards of the organization, that is, its rules of discourse, while strategic and tactical changes involve revision at the level of the abstract solution.

Like writers, program designers make many notes. This is linked to the iterative nature of the process and to the limited capacity of the working memory, whence the need for an external memory. It is also linked to the need to for maintenance programmers to be able to understand why a particular design was adopted.

Software designers produce a large number of notes in natural language while they are designing their programs: design notes, temporary comments or comments that will remain in the final program[28]. Even though the final goal of the design process is to produce a list of instructions coded in a programming language, information expressed in natural language forms an integral part of the design process and of the solution produced.

Various authors[29] have analysed the nature of the natural language information produced during design. Designers use a design notebook to make notes in temporary memory in the course of design. Designers produce notes at different levels of abstraction, from justification of high level design decisions down to implementation details. If they are asked to produce only one type of note on a particular field of the environment, they often deviate from the prescribed category and mix in several types of information.

This behaviour is interpreted as reflecting the iterative and interactive nature of the design process[30]. The different types of information produced are narrowly connected to the designers' representations not on the basis of their syntactic or

---

[c]In this sense, the model incorporates the opportunistic aspect of design organization.

semantic status, but on the basis of the sub-problem that is being treated at a given moment. Some notes serve simply as external memory and will be deleted subsequently, e.g. the consequence that a design decision has on a sub-problem that will be dealt with later. Other note, e.g. the rationale for certain design decisions, will remain in the program or its documentation as an aid to the human reader.

This intense notetaking activity, which one can describe as the use of external memory, seems to be linked to expertise and has been analysed[31] within the framework of display-based problem solving. It should be noted that, once it is recorded externally, the code itself can be considered as forming part of an external memory[32].

3.5 Modelling the Expert

What distinguishes the expert from the novice? What are the stages on the road to acquiring expertise? Can we distinguish several types of expertise? Research is able to provide at least some answers to questions of this type.

3.5.1 What Distinguishes an Expert from a Novice?

Organization of Knowledge

In the field of computing, as in other fields such as chess or physics, experts form abstract, conceptual representations of problems while novices represent the problems in terms of surface features. Experts possess hierarchically organized knowledge, which gives them a better processing capacity than novices. This is consistent with the knowledge centred approach. Two experimental paradigms have allowed the organization of knowledge by experts and novices in the programming field to be compared: the understanding/recall paradigm and the categorization paradigm.

The understanding/recall paradigm is illustrated by an experiment[33] in which subjects were presented with programs, some of which had the lines of code in the correct order and some of which had the lines in random order. The subjects were then asked to recall the programs. The recall of the experts was better than that of the novices when the lines were in the correct order but not when they were in random order. In the second case, no significant structures could be identified.

The categorization paradigm consists in presenting to programmers a certain number of programs or fragments of programs and asking them to categorize them and explain their categorization criteria. In this way, it can be shown[34] that the categories formed by expert programmers are different from those formed by novices. While the categories formed by the novices depend on the surface features of programs, e.g. the syntactic structure, the categories formed by the experts revealed deeper structures such as functional or procedural similarity.

The multi-dimensional nature of program design expertise needs to be underlined[35]. Knowledge in the following areas is important: general computing knowledge, specialized design schemas, software engineering techniques, knowledge of more technical domains such as knowledge of programming environments, and knowledge of the application or problem domain. On this last point, there has been little work done on expertise in the application domain and its role in programming activities. Some recent studies have shown the importance of such knowledge both in the design and the understanding of programs[36].

Strategies and Use of Knowledge

A complementary approach to the characterization of expertise is to consider whether experts are distinguished not only by possessing more and better organized knowledge than novices but also by their better capacity to use the knowledge[37] they have. This is consistent with the strategy-centred approach and with the organization-centred approach.

Research has shown that, compared with novices,

- experts construct a more complete problem representation before embarking on the process of solving it[38];
- they use more rules of discourse[39]. Recall that such rules govern the instantiation of knowledge schemas during design (see Section 3.2.5);
- they use more meta-cognitive knowledge about programming tasks and about suitable and optimal strategies for completing them[40]. They know a number of possible strategies for completing a task and are able to compare them with a view to selecting the optimal strategy for that task;
- they are capable of generating several alternative solutions before making a choice[41];
- they use more external devices, particularly as external memory[42];
- their design strategy is top-down and forward for familiar and not too complex problems[43], while that novices is bottom-up and backward;
- some aspects of programming tasks are carried out completely automatically[44].

3.5.2 Can Different Levels of Expertise Be Distinguished?

A number of writers[45] have remarked upon the existence of 'super experts' or 'exceptional designers' in software development teams. What distinguishes these super-experts, as they are known by their peers, from other experts? The following characteristics have been identified:

- a broader rather than longer experience: the number of projects in which they have been involved, the number and variety of the programming languages they know;
- technical and computing knowledge;
- a particular ability to combine computing knowledge with knowledge of the application domain;
- social skills such as communication and co-operation.

3.5.3 What Are the Stages in Acquiring Expertise?

Three stages have been recognised in building up knowledge schemas[46]:

- construction of elementary programming schemas;
- construction of complex programming schemas;
- converting the internal structure of schemas into a hierarchy by abstraction from the focal point.

Knowledge of the roles or structural schemas is acquired very early and provides the skeleton on which knowledge schemas are constructed.

Experienced programmers retrieve complex schemas when they have relatively simple problems to program, while novices build these schemas. The retrieval of schemas manifests itself in the fact that the actions of the schema are developed in the canonical order of the schema, which is also the order of execution. In other words, when the programmer has a general solution schema, the program is constructed top-down and in a forward direction.

Internal restructuring of schemas takes place during the acquisition of expertise. From this angle, expertise is built up through the development of hierarchically structured schemas; the focus, that part of the schema that directly implements its goal, becomes hierarchically superior to the other parts of the schema. The focus is then a more prominent part and thus more readily available in memory. In a preliminary scan of memory, depending on the level of expertise, this part is more rapidly recognized than other parts of the schema. In fact, this effect is observed among experts, but not among novice or intermediate programmers.

This work is limited because into fails to take into account the acquisition processes that lead to changes in the organisation of knowledge in the course of acquiring expertise, e.g. the processes of generalization, specialization and proceduralization[47]. Further, it does not take account of the acquisition of knowledge about the conditions under which a schema is applicable. Given a problem, such knowledge allows the designer to select a number of candidate schemas and choose between them. This aspect of acquiring expertise has been studied in tasks such as editing[48] but not in programming.

3.6 Making Tools More Suitable for Programmers

Implementation and Visualization of Schemas

Structural schemas and knowledge schemas can be provided to the designer as aids to program design.

In no case does the notion of a structural schema reduce to the purely syntactic aspects of a language. Present day structural editors are, however, based on the syntax of a language, and often on its control structure. Different levels of nesting in the control structure are distinguished, which, in software engineering, provides a basis for assessing the complexity of a program. From an ergonomic point of view, it would be more useful to provide tools based on the notion of a structural schema. The tools might operate on two levels:

- at the level of a knowledge base. This would provide structural schemas suitable for certain languages or certain programming paradigms. These structural schemas could be provided on demand, to help in structuring programs. For example, to help in designing object-oriented programs, we might provide structural object schemas, associating with a generic object the following generic roles and functions: creation, initialization, read access, write access, inputs, outputs;

- at the level of visualization of these structural schemas in a program being written. This would allow the program to be described at a level relatively independent of the syntax and control structure of the language.

Knowledge schemas could also be made available to designers, to assist them in their search for solutions. This could again be done on two levels:

- the knowledge base. This would provide knowledge schemas suitable for handling certain problems[d]. Taking inspiration from the approach in terms of programming schemas, described in Section 3.2.2, one could formalize both the elementary programming schemas and the complex ones, and characterize the different types of links (composition, specialization, and use) between them. It would be useful to add:
  - information on the use and validity conditions of the programming schemas, e.g. limiting cases;
  - examples of instantiation of the schemas;
  - alternative schemas for the same problem, taking us back to the specialization and use links;

- visualization of programming schemas in a program being written. It is a characteristic of complex programming schemas that they are instantiated in a dispersed manner. In other words, the instructions belonging to a single schema are not contiguous in the program but can belong to different parts. For example, the initialization line and the update line of a counter variable plan are not contiguous in the program code. This feature may explain certain programming errors, especially ones due to forgetfulness. A tool to display instances of schemas[e] would be particularly useful since it would allow semantically connected but non-contiguous elements of the code to be grouped together visually.

More generally, it seems very useful to allow designers to visualize the different types of relation that exist in a program as well as putting them into correspondence one with another. From this point of view, it has been suggested that software development environments should support multiple views of the system, such as control flow, data flow, and functional decomposition. We shall return to this point in Chapter 7, on understanding programs.

---

[d]The work on design patterns (Gamma, Helm, Johnson and Vlissides, 1994) seems a promising way forward here.
[e]The plans representing elements of a single schema could be traced and identified according to Rist (1994), on the basis of data flow analysis. But this means that the program must be complete and not in the course of construction.

Implementation of Design Strategies

We have identified different dimensions that characterize design strategies: bottom-up vs top-down development, forward vs backward, procedural vs declarative. It has been suggested[49] that support might be provided for strategies varying according to the first two of these dimensions. While top-down strategies are often supported – or indeed, enforced – by programming environments, bottom-up strategies and their linking with top-down strategies are rarely, if ever, supported. As far as the second dimension is concerned, support for backward development is provided by certain environments such as MAIDAY[50] but support for a forward strategy seems much more difficult to implement, because the goals of the designer are more difficult to infer than the prerequisites of explicitly stated goals. On this last point, it seems to us possible to envisage some support for a forward strategy, provided that it is not based solely on the code but uses also a more abstract definition of the solution, produced by the designer. Further, some help with simulation should be provided because this activity, particularly useful for debugging (see Chapter 7), is often a source of errors.

Opportunistic Design

The emphasis on the opportunistic nature of design has made the designers of programming environments conscious of the serious constraints that they place on programmers by imposing a top-down approach. Recent articles[51] bear witness to the desire to allow for design organized in a more opportunistic fashion. This means, on the one hand, not restricting the development to being completely top-down and breadth-first, and, on the other hand, supporting opportunistic activity through tools that allow the solution plan to be managed so as to warn of errors and omissions caused by opportunistic deviations. We can illustrate these two aspects by considering two tools, HoodNICE[f] and ReuseNICE[52], intended to support design and reuse. They are based on the HOOD (Hierarchical Object Oriented Design) method, which is purely top-down, but allow the following opportunistic deviations:

- the breadth-first decomposition strategy defined by the HOOD method can be interrupted to allow tactically better choices to be followed;
- the HoodNICE editor was modified to allow bottom-up development as well as top-down. In particular, a child object can be created before its parent;
- several levels of the design tree can be displayed and edited at the same time;
- the solution can be temporarily inconsistent with the rules defined by the method (e.g. naming rules, order of definition of code entities). An off-line checker is available when required, to check for inconsistencies;
- notes concerning, for example, consequences of decisions taken and how they affect later tasks can be made and stored in a work book.

---

[f]HoodNICE was developed by Intecs Sistemi and its ergonomic evaluation was carried out as part of the European SCALE (System Composition and Large Grain Component Reuse Support) project. See Oquendo, Détienne, Gallo, Kastner and Martelli, 1993.

Finally, it has been suggested that, in order to support opportunistic activity, the designer might be provided with a representation of the solution plan, which would help to identify incomplete tasks or tasks put on one side as a result of side tracking. Such support can be envisaged at the level of the process model, which would make it relatively independent of the programming environment.

Teaching Tools

A learning model that takes account of the process of acquiring knowledge schemas, as in Soloway's approach, has given rise to teaching tools based on the idea of programming schemas. The underlying hypothesis is that presenting and teaching the schemas to beginners will help them to develop expertise[53].

As a complement to this, according to an acquisition model in terms of internal restructuring of schemas, one might think that practice with structured programming and, more generally, training in design would facilitate the development of expertise. This would focus beginners' attention on the important parts of the schema and thus encourage them to restructure the schema hierarchically.

While the validity of the first approach has still to be conclusively proved, the second has hardly been tested experimentally[g]; the one study of which we are aware[54] shows that, for a given amount of practical experience, training in structured programming leads to better performance than a more classical training. One limit of these approaches is that they do not help to build strategic knowledge, which is just as important as generic knowledge of solutions.

3.7 Future Research

One direction for future research is the analysis of the subjects' understanding of the problem to be solved. In every study of program design, the same implicit assumption is made: the subjects will all have constructed the same representation of the problem. This is manifestly false when the problem to be solved is non-trivial. Much of the variability between individuals observed in studies of the design process might be explained by this.

Another direction is to analyse further the design strategies and the organization of the design activity, and to take more detailed account of the conditions under which they are adopted. From a theoretical point of view, the objective would be to build a model that integrates the different design approaches. We have already seen that they are, in practice, complementary and this fact deserves to be more widely recognized and better articulated.

Finally, so far as the acquisition of expertise is concerned, the mechanism for constructing knowledge at present envisaged is extremely simplified since it is limited to a mechanism for acquiring knowledge schemas. It would be useful to go further in the analysis of these acquisition mechanisms. The analysis of the

---

[g]Both approaches are, of course, widely used in teaching programming and software design and widely believed to be superior to other approaches. All that is being asserted here is that there is little scientific evidence, based on properly designed experiments, to demonstrate this superiority[53].

mechanisms for reorganizing this knowledge as well as of the mechanisms for constructing knowledge about schemas are the path along which research might proceed.

References

1. Hoc, 1984a; 1987b.
2. Adelson, 1981, 1984; Black, Kay and Soloway, 1986; Détienne, 1990b, 1990c. Détienne and Soloway, 1990; Rist, 1986, 1989, 1991; Robertson, 1990; Soloway, Erhlich and Bonar, 1982a; Soloway, Erhlich, Bonar and Greenspan, 1982b; Soloway and Ehrlich, 1984.
3. Soloway, Erhlich and Bonar, 1982a.
4. Soloway and Ehrlich, 1984.
5. Visser and Hoc, 1990.
6. See, for example, the papers from the two product line sessions in ICSE (2000).
7. Hoc, 1987b.
8. Rist, 1991.
9. Wirth, 1974.
10. Adelson and Soloway, 1985.
11. Green, 1989, 1990; Green and Petre, 1996.
12. Davies, 1991.
13. Green, Bellamy and Parker, 1987.
14. Détienne, 1990a; 1990d.
15. Hoc, 1981.
16. Détienne, 1995; Chatel and Détienne, 1996.
17. Reference required.
18. Rist, 1991.
19. Adelson and Soloway, 1985, 1988; Carroll, Thomas and Malhotra, 1979; Guindon and Curtis, 1988; Jeffries, Turner, Polson and Atwood, 1981.
20. Adelson and Soloway, 1985.
21. Guindon, Krasner and Curtis, 1987; Guindon, 1990a; Visser, 1987.
22. Jeffries, Turner, Polson and Atwood, 1981; Visser, 1987.
23. Davies and Castell, 1994.
24. Visser, 1994a, 1994b.
25. Hayes and Flower, 1980.
26. Bereiter, Burtis and Scardamalia, 1988.
27. Gray and Anderson, 1987.
28. Bellamy, 1994a; Davies, 1996; Henry, Green, Gilmore and Davies, 1992.
29. Détienne, Rouet, Burkhardt and Deleuze-Dordron, 1996; Rouet, Deleuze-Dordron & Bisseret, 1995a, 1995b.
30. Détienne, Rouet, Burkhardt and Deleuze-Dordron, 1996.
31. Davies, 1996.
32. Green, Bellamy and Parker, 1987.
33. Shneiderman, 1976.
34. Adelson, 1981, 1985.
35. Guindon and Curtis, 1988.
36. Shaft and Vessey, 1995; Sharp 1991.
37. Davies, 1993a; Gilmore, 1990.
38. Batra and Davies, 1992.
39. Davies, 1990a.
40. Eteläpelto, 1993.
41. Guindon, Krasner and Curtis, 1987; Jeffries, Turner, Polson and Atwood, 1981; Visser, 1994a.
42. Davies, 1996.
43. Adelson and Soloway, 1988; Rist, 1991.
44. Wiedenbeck, 1985.
45. Curtis, Krasner and Iscoe, 1988; Sheppard, Curtis, Milliman and Love, 1979; Sonnentag, 1995, 1996.
46. Davies, 1994; Rist, 1991.
47. Rumelhart and Norman, 1978.
48. Black, Kay and Soloway, 1986.
49. Visser and Hoc, 1990.

50. Guyard and Jacquot, 1984; Hoc, 1988.
51. Bisseret, Deleuze-Dordron, Détienne and Rouet, 1995; Guindon and Curtis, 1988; Guindon, 1992; Visser and Hoc, 1990.
52. D'Alessandro and Martelli, 1994.
53. Anderson, Boyle, Farrel and Reisner, 1987; Bonar and Cunningham, 1988.
54. Davies, 1990b, 1993b.

4. *Software Reuse*

■ ■

The work presented in the previous chapter was centred around the reasoning process that leads to the development of solutions, with the accent on generic knowledge stored in memory. It is limited in that it takes little account of the way in which previous solutions are exploited in the course of design. However, the design of a computing system is a task that rarely results in an original solution. The development of a solution is often based not only on generic knowledge but also on the retrieval of external or internal characteristics of particular solutions developed for analogous problems: on these grounds, it can be said to involve as much the reuse of solutions already known[1] as creation of new ones. The work on opportunism in program development, described in the previous chapter, has brought to light certain phenomena involving the reuse of solutions and the use of reasoning by analogy. More quantitative studies[a] show the importance of reuse in program design.

Software reuse goes back to the earliest days of computing; a library of reusable subroutines was developed for the EDSAC 1 computer in Cambridge in the early 1950s. Such libraries became part of the software that was bundled in with hardware purchases. Another form of software reuse was the program generator, a program to generate other programs – sort programs, report writing programs, compilers, etc. These developments were driven largely by commercial considerations; the term software reuse was unknown. Interest in software reuse per se was sparked off by a much cited paper[2] delivered by McIlroy at a NATO conference in 1968. The 1970s saw the development of substantial libraries of reusable components for such areas as graphics and numerical analysis, as well as portable systems software such as real time executives and database management systems. The promotion of reuse was a significant factor in the design of the programming language Ada in the late 1970s. As the so-called software crisis became more acute during the 1980s, software reuse was increasingly seen as the key to resolving it. The enormous increase in processing power has led to comparable increases in software complexity, in the user interface, for example. This has led, in turn, to today's designers being offered libraries of software components that are very much larger than those previously available. For the first time the size of the libraries has become a barrier to their effective use.

---

[a]Kamath and Smith (1992) report that, with the use of C++, in a project traditionally implemented in the C language, 72 per cent of the classes in the first version of the application were reused in the second version.

Current tools (e.g. libraries, search utilities) try to help designers by allowing them to retrieve the components or solutions[b] from a library and by minimizing the size of the modifications needed to integrate the component into the application being developed. From this point of view, the object-oriented paradigm is often presented as offering a high level of reuse. Nevertheless, the few empirical studies on reuse in programming show that the tools we have for locating and selecting reusable elements are a long way from satisfying the needs of designers or being compatible with the way they go about their activities.

In this chapter we shall first present, in Section 4.2, a theoretical framework suitable for studying software reuse: analogical reasoning models. Section 4.3 will be devoted to an analysis of the different cognitive mechanisms involved in the activity of software reuse and to the ergonomic implications of this analysis. In Section 4.4, we shall present a cognitive classification of reuse situations and their practical implications. We shall finish the chapter by looking at different research perspectives.

■ ■

4.1 Analogical Reasoning Models

We shall give a brief presentation of the main analogical reasoning models as they have been developed in cognitive psychology. These models offer a theoretical framework suitable for studying the cognitive mechanisms of reuse. The reuse of solutions in program design uses, *inter alia*, the mechanisms classically studied under the theme of analogical reasoning: understanding of the target situation, retrieval of a source situation[c], mapping between source and target. However, studies of analogical reasoning have often been mainly concerned with the mechanisms of source utilization, that is, the use of sources constructed by the experimenter and made available to the subjects for solving target problems. A special aspect of the reuse situation in programming is that the sources have been constructed previously by the designer himself or by other designers expert in the area, and that, in a natural design situation, they are not provided directly to the designer but must be retrieved by him or her. Another special aspect of the situation is that it involves design problems for which there exist different and alternative solutions and for which the problem constraints are badly defined; this is not the case in the majority of the problem solving situations used in studies of reasoning by analogy.

4.1.1 The Syntactic Model and the Pragmatic Model

Two major phases are distinguished in the study of reasoning by analogy: access and use. In the access phase, a source situation is selected or retrieved from

---

[b]These solutions may be at the level of analysis, specification or implementation.
[c]It should be noted that, in computing, the component retrieved is often called the target component for reuse. We shall adopt the terminology used in analogical reasoning models, that is to say we shall use the term *source* to designate the analogous situation retrieved to handle the current problem situation, which we shall call the *target situation*.

memory. In the use phase, the source situation is applied to the current target situation. More precisely, we distinguish:

- the construction of a representation of the target situation;
- retrieval or selection of a source situation analogous to the target situation;
- mapping between the source situation and the target situation;
- adaptation of the source solution to solve the target problem.

According to the syntactic model[3], the mapping between the source and the target is based on an abstract structure common to the two situations. According to the pragmatic model[4], this mapping is carried out only between problems having the same goals and with the same underlying solution structure. Studies show that the use of analogical reasoning is not, in general, spontaneous. Access to an analog may be based on a surface similarity between the two situations, a structural similarity, or a similarity of goals[5]. But surface similarity plays a significant role in triggering reasoning by analogy.

Two limitations of these models should be underlined. First, they analyse access as a process of matching between a source and a target. In the experimental situations studied, the source situation is often supplied to the subject. This can be criticized in two ways. From one point of view, the external validity of the situations studied by the authors is weak in relation to natural problem solving situations, where a potentially large number of source situations may have to be searched for and retrieved before being used. From another point of view, the models of access are viewed within a theoretical framework influenced by models of memory access: thus it is assumed that a representation of the source is already stored in memory prior to its use for reasoning by analogy. We shall see, however, that the source situation can be constructed through reasoning by analogy just as well as the target situation.

A second limitation is that these models offer only a limited role to schemas in the process of reasoning by analogy. In general, they consider the construction of a schema as a process resulting from the use of reasoning by analogy and hence from the treatment of several analogous situations which can be considered as different instances of the same schema. In the situation called 'reasoning from an analog', the target problem is mapped directly to a source situation to generate a solution[6]. A schema, an abstract representation common to two analogs, does not exist as an individual concept in memory prior to the reasoning. On the other hand, the induction of a schema can be a process resulting from this mapping. In the situation called 'reasoning from a schema', which relates to the situations analysed in the previous chapter, a schema has already been constructed as a result of the treatment of analogous situations in the past and this schema is stored in memory. If the new situation lends itself to the application of this schema, the designer can reason directly from the schema and specialize it to process a new instance. In this case, there is no reasoning by analogy.

To sum up, these models do not consider the role of schemas, properly so called, in the mechanisms of reasoning by analogy. It seems that, even in situations where a schema already exists in memory, reasoning by analogy may be used based on this schema and on one or several analogs which would be instances of the schema developed in the past: for example, we shall see that access to an analog can be based on the activation of a schema common to the source and target situations.

4.1.2 Clement's Model

Clement's model[7] allows the preceding criticisms to be addressed and offers a more adequate theoretical framework for studying reuse in natural problem solving situations and, notably, in design. Clement distinguishes the following processes in reasoning by analogy:

1. *Generate an analog.* A source situation, which is potentially analogous to the target situation is generated. A provisional analogical relationship between the two situations is established. This process of generation can rest on the following mechanisms:

   - generation of an analog starting from a formal principle (or schema) or retrieval of an example via a schema. In this case, the activation of a formal principle that is suitable for handling the target problem is followed by accessing an example of the principle. Thus the generation of a source situation, an instance of a schema, is carried out by activating the schema;
   - generation of an analog by transforming the target situation. In this case, the experimental subject creates an analogous source situation by transforming the target situation, e.g. by modifying various characteristics of this situation. There is then no recourse to an abstract principle or schema;
   - generation by an association between the source and the target. In this case, the target situation reminds the subject of an analogous situation.

2. *Build up confidence in the analogical relationship.* The validity of the relationship between the source and the target is examined critically and is confirmed or not. One way of doing this is to construct a 'bridging analogy', that is, an analogical case intermediate between the source and the target. Other ways include 'matching key relationships' and finding a 'conserving transformation'.

3. *Understand the analogical case.* The designer examines and, if necessary, develops a deeper understanding of the source so that its behaviour is well understood.

4. *Apply the results.* The designer applies to the target situation the conclusions and methods that have come out of the source situation.

Clement's model is based on the analysis of scientific problem solving situations where the source is not presented directly to the designer. From this point of view it has considerable experimental validity. In this more natural context, it can be shown that the source situation itself may be constructed during the course of the analogical reasoning, something that is not envisaged in the syntactic and pragmatic models. Clement's model also brings a new clarity to the role of schemas (called concepts or abstract principles by Clement) in reasoning by analogy. It demonstrates clearly that this type of reasoning can be based at the same time on a schema and one or more analogs or instances of the schema.

4.2 Cognitive Mechanisms Employed in Reuse

We shall analyse the cognitive mechanisms employed in software reuse by distinguishing two phases: the generation of the source and the use of the source.

4.2.1 Generation of a Source

Retrieval Based on Examples vs Retrieval Based on Formal Attributes

It is generally understood by the computing community that it is always necessary to organize and present reusable components in a formal and abstract manner. Empirical studies, however, show the importance of strongly contextualized examples[8]. Memory retrieval mechanisms favour the use of examples as index terms rather than generic attributes, e.g. in the task of eliciting examples of natural categories or the task of architectural design. A tendency has been observed among students to think initially in terms of concrete solutions and of images retrieved from memory, rather than in terms of instantiations of constraints on the design space. The preponderance of highly contextualized indices has also been noted[9] in a program design task, when experts are searching for reusable components.

Retrieval is often a question of recourse to strongly contextualized personal (i.e. episodic) knowledge, in other words, the designer has been in a very similar situation before. In some cases, such as a task involving the retrieval and elicitation of different examples of categories, this tendency has been found to be very marked but in others the association with a personal reference appears in less than half the cases.

Retrieval based on examples illustrates the operation of different kinds of knowledge:

- the reuse of instances of schemas: in this case the example is an instance of a schema kept in memory;
- the reuse of episodic knowledge concerning, for example, an application developed in the past:
  - the application is an analogous case for which a schema has not previously been constructed. The construction of the schema can, on the other hand, be the result of reasoning by analogy;
  - certain aspects of the application illustrate forms of specialization of the schemas. The application knowledge provides, on the one hand, an index for retrieving from memory these schema instances and, on the other hand, contextual information about the implementation of these schemas.

Retrieval of an Instance Via a Schema

Burkhardt (1997) presents two situations in which program designers retrieve an instance of a schema as source:

- a schema or abstract principle judged suitable for handling the target situation is recalled and the designer also recalls for this purpose one or several instances of this schema developed in the past;

- a schema that is not completely applicable to the target situation is recalled and again the designer also recalls one or several instances of this schema developed in the past. It is clear then that the source situation recalled brings into play solution principles quite different from the target situation but that the designer will all the same examine whether certain aspects can be retrieved and used to handle the target situation.

Construction of an Instance Via a Schema

Another way[10] in which schemas are used in reasoning by analogy involves the construction of an instance of a schema that will serve as a source for an episode of such reasoning. In the course of developing a single program, the designer may judge that one part of the solution that is being developed can be reused to develop other parts of the solution. In this situation, referred to as 'new code reuse', the different parts of the solution can be considered to be different instances of the same schema. Designers explained, for example, that several instances of a schema to search for objects would need to be developed for different programming objects. Thus the generation of the source is carried out by constructing an instance of a schema; in our example, the first instance of the schema 'search for objects' that is developed will have the status of the source. We shall see in Section 4.3.1 that this situation, reuse of new code, is characterized by mechanisms of anticipation and mechanisms involving the reorganization of the design activity.

Generation of a Source by Modifying the Representation of the Target Problem and Constructing Intermediate Situations

Burkhardt and Détienne observe that experts use two ways of describing reusable components:

- direct description, i.e. the description of the functions and properties of the reusable components;
- description in terms of behaviour, i.e., the reusable components are mainly described through the behaviour that will result from including them in the target solution.

This second style of description appears almost systematically in the linguistic conventions of the designers. According to Clement's model, it could be interpreted as the construction of an intermediate situation resulting from the generation of a source by the modification of the representation of the target situation.

Iterative Searching

Searching for knowledge in memory is an iterative process[11]. The specifications of the element sought are often incomplete and they are refined bit by bit on the basis of knowledge retrieved by an iterative search process. Although, so far as we know, there have been no empirical studies on software reuse that address this question, it is likely that the same type of iterative process is employed in searching for reusable components in a library.

4.2.2 Use of the Source

Enriching the Representation of the Target Situation

The information retrieved from a source situation allows the representation of the target situation to be enriched. This enrichment can take a variety of forms such as addition of constraints, addition of goals, or use of validation criteria to assess the target situation.

The retrieval of a source situation leads the program designer to became aware of new design constraints[d]. These constraints are then transferred to the representation of the target situation and thus allow this representation to be enriched. The same effect has been observed in architectural design[12]. Architects are provided with a large number of examples presented on three levels of a concrete/abstract axis. It is then observed that, on the one hand, the designers add new constraints to the problem representation and, on the other hand, that the level at which the target situation constraints already identified are considered becomes significantly more abstract.

Software reuse involves top-down processes, such as refinement of the target solution, that are classically expected in reuse activities, but also bottom-up processes, such as the generation of new goals, that were not previously expected in the design activity[13]. These ascending processes are manifested in the construction of a more abstract representation of the target situation and in the addition of goals to this abstract representation of the solution. In one experiment, it was observed that, out of the total number of elements mentioned during reuse, almost half correspond to the introduction of goals that were not initially explicit.

Assessment and Revision of the Target

The retrieval of information on the context of a preceding problem used as an analog provides criteria for judging how well the source solution will satisfy the requirements of the target problem. Designers recall validation criteria linked to the context in which the source component was previously employed, this context being adjudged similar to the target context. These criteria are used in order to assess the validity of the component for the target solution, possibly calling into question all or part of the target solution developed earlier.

4.2.3 Implications

Nature and Organization of the Reusable Components

As well as episodic knowledge of applications, schemas and instances of schemas are exploited in the reuse activity. A library of reusable components should formalize these three types of knowledge and provide links between them. This would:

- provide two different ways of searching the library: by formal attributes describing the schemas or by contextual information describing the episodic

---

[d]The notion of constraint is seen here as a dependency relation between at least two variables. See, for example, Darses (1992).

knowledge (instances or applications). This also provides different retrieval modes for schemas and instances of schemas. For example:

- the subject retrieves a schema and has the option of also retrieving different instances of the schema;
- the subject retrieves an application and can retrieve all the instances of schemas implemented in this application, as well as the corresponding schemas themselves;

• allow the retrieval of knowledge of different kinds linked to the reusable components chosen: validity criteria, problem constraints, context of use, etc.

Support for Bottom-up and Top-down Processes

Like prescriptive design methods of the hierarchical type, models of reuse usually advocate a top-down approach. Empirical studies, however, show that reuse involves both top-down and bottom-up processes. Thus, sometimes a component can be retrieved and judged adequate for a sub-problem which it won't actually handle: the sub-problem may be too detailed in comparison with the level of detail currently being considered or, on the other hand, at too high a level of abstraction. In such cases, it may be useful to keep a record of this choice of component even if the designer doesn't want to use it in the development process immediately. The provision of a 're-use notebook' as a means of storing these selections would help to support both top-down and bottom-up reuse. This idea has been implemented in the ReuseNICE tool (D'Alessandro and Martelli, 1994).

Another bottom-up process implied by reuse is the restructuring of the solution at a level of abstraction higher than the current one. For this process, bottom-up program editors would provide valuable support.

Support for Constructing Intermediate Situations

Studies of reasoning by analogy show that designers sometimes construct situations that are intermediate between the target situation and the source. These are linking analogs that allow analogs in between the source and the target to be envisaged. Such a construction allows confidence in the analogical relationship to be established. The construction of intermediate situations might be supported by providing the designer with a work area separate from that used for developing the target situation.

Use of Examples

In the reuse of software components contextual information could be provided to the designers in the form of examples of applications developed in the past that incorporate the reusable components. This would support the process of retrieval by example. Further, rather than search for each component individually in the library, the designer would in this way retrieve a set of reusable components for an analogous application and would be able to make a selection from among them. This would thus help with the process of using components on the basis of contextual information.

Support for Iterative Searching

The search for reusable components is iterative. The paradigm of retrieval by reformulation[14] can help with such searches. An initial request, which is typically incomplete, is formulated and this request can be refined little by little on the basis of the information retrieved from the component library.

To conclude, it seems to us important to emphasize that the activity of reuse requires a specific skill, distinct from programming skills or expertise in the application domain. Designers with little experience in reuse have been shown[15] to have difficulty assessing the reusability of a component they have not designed in the context of a target problem. Effectively they base their choices on irrelevant features of the components, such as their size; rather than relevant ones, such as the estimated number of changes to be carried out. A survey of the use of a reuse environment[16] has also shown clearly that experienced programmers, even ones who are expert in the application domain, have serious difficulties when learning to use such a tool. They lack the techniques for selecting and using reusable components. It seems necessary, therefore, to learn such techniques and be trained in reuse, as well as in the tools provided to support the activity.

4.3 Cognitive Classification of Reuse Situations

One classification that is currently used in software engineering is based on the type of the component, reused, with which is associated a preferred type of activity. It distinguishes the extraction of code from an existing application (for example, lines of codes or procedures), specialization of components, generally taken from a library, and finally inheritance/composition of classes. For each of these situations, reuse is associated with modifications at different levels. Two other axes can be used to construct a cognitive classification of reuse situations: the type of the reuse instance ('reuse of new code' as against 'reuse of old code') and the design phase during which the reuse takes place (reuse in the course of analysis, searching for a solution, or coding). These axes are orthogonal to the axis characterizing the type of the component. This cognitive classification allows some of the cognitive mechanisms belonging to certain situations to be identified:

- mechanisms of preparing for the task and reorganizing it, belonging to the situation of reusing new code ;

- mechanisms for enriching the representation of the target when practising reuse during analysis and solution searching or, at the other extreme, lowering the level of control[e] of the activity when reusing during coding.

---

[e]We refer to the hierarchy of control levels developed by Rasmussen and Lind (1982). These authors distinguish automatic mental activities, mental activities based on rules, and mental activities that put high level knowledge to work. The lowering of the control level of an activity means moving from mental activities based on high level knowledge, e.g. problem solving activities, to activities based on rules and automatics activities, e.g. executing procedures.

4.3.1 Reuse of New Code vs Reuse of Old Code

One way of classifying reuse depends on whether the reuse episode begins with the development of the code (new code reuse) or not (old code reuse).

As an example of new code reuse, consider the case of a designer designing an appointments system for a doctor's surgery. He or she quickly recognizes the need to be able to calculate the date of the day immediately following a given one. In the course of developing a solution to this (not totally trivial) problem, it becomes apparent that this solution will help to solve the problem of calculating the date of the day a week or a month after a given date, a problem that occurs elsewhere in the system. The designer therefore tries to formulate the solution in a way that can be reused in solving these other problems. In practice, this will probably mean writing a function that takes two parameters, a date and an integer, and returns the date that is the integer number of days after the date supplied.

More abstractly, we can say that, in the course of designing a piece of software, the designer develops a solution to a sub-problem (which will have the status of the source) and envisages reusing it to solve other sub-problems that are still to come (which will have the status of targets). A cognitive process peculiar to this situation is the process of looking ahead while developing the source. In effect, the designer anticipates the way that the source will be adapted to construct the target solutions. This mechanism manifests itself in two forms:

- construction of an operative representation of the source, that is, one which distinguishes clearly between the fixed features of the source and the features that may be varied when it is reused;
- construction of an adaptation procedure from the source to the targets; this adaptation procedure allows the variable parts to be modified in order to create other instances of the same schema.

Another cognitive mechanism peculiar to this situation is reorganization of the design activity. If, in the original plan, different elements that are considered to be instances of a single schema are scheduled to be developed at widely separated times during the design, the designer will reorganize the plan in order to develop these instances in a block. This allows the representation of the source and the adaptation procedure to be kept in working memory, without adding representation constructed in the course of other development activities. It thus minimizes the risk of errors of omission.

When reusing old code, the designer retrieves and adapts a solution previously developed for a problem analogous to the one in question. This situation implies that the mechanisms used relate to the retrieval of a source and the exploration of the relationship between the source and the target, in order to develop the new solution.

4.3.2 Reuse During the Different Design Phases

Reuse in the problem analysis phase, reuse in the design phase and reuse in the implementation phase are all different.

Reuse during the problem analysis phase has the effect of enriching the representation of target situation. Retrieving reusable components, particularly examples, adds extra constraints to the representation[17]. It has been observed[18] that designers, starting from an analogous example, infer new specifications for the target problem. Thus, sometimes, even when the reusable component is defined at code level, the code retrieved is not exploited as such but as a functional specification. A common example of this is when the designer retrieves a component that provides functions for searching a table. While the functions it provides may well be exactly what is required in the target solution, the algorithms used may be unsuitable for performance reasons, because of the relative frequency of updates compared to retrievals for example. This results in new performance constraints being added to the target representation.

Reuse when searching for a design solution also has the effect of enriching the representation of the target situation. A reusable component can serve as a guide for the solving the current problem by suggesting alternative solutions, solution plans, or criteria for evaluating alternative solutions[19]. The retrieval of reusable components leads the designer to recall validity criteria linked to the context in which the reusable component has previously been used, this context being considered similar to the target context. The information recalled is used to judge the appropriateness of the component to the target situation.

Reuse during implementation allows the level of control of the activity to be lowered. The designer chooses a design solution that he tries to implement by reusing a component that can be fitted into his solution, give or take a few modifications. The lowering of the level of control manifests itself in (1) the use of an operative representation of the source in episodes involving the reuse of new code and (2) the use of a trial and error strategy[20].

A trial and error strategy involves copying and modifying code. Designers tend to reuse code by copying it and making the modifications that they judge the most likely. They try to avoid understanding the source code (a strategy known as comprehension avoidance), by depending on surface features to form hypotheses about its functionality. They then rely on the test and debugging tools at their disposal to modify and correct the code in order to adapt it to the target situation. We note that this strategy is encouraged, if not, indeed, dictated by, the tools available: debugging tools are currently much better developed than tools to help understanding, e.g. suitable documentation.

4.3.3 Implications

Our cognitive classification of reuse situations allows us to suggest different reuse aids. Different types of reuse episode require different types of support. For episodes involving the reuse of new code, support for the visualization of the operative representation of the source and the construction of the modification procedure, constructed in this situation, would be useful. Such assistance could form the basis for the automatic generation of target systems. Further, it would be useful to support the debugging of the different instances produced in the course of the same episode of reusing new code. This is the case when an error is found in one of the instances; the correction must first be introduced into this instance and then propagated to the others. A computer-based mechanism to find all the instances generated in the same episode would save time and avoid omissions. For episodes involving the reuse of old code, support for the retrieval and under-standing of source situations needs to be considered.

Reuse at different stages of the development process changes the cognitive status of the element reused and hence calls for different ways of supporting the under-standing of the source.

Depending on the type of activity in which the designer is engaged, the type of information sought in the reusable element varies (constraints in the specifi-cation, design model, element to be included) and the support needed is not therefore of the same type. On this last point, it seems that offering several types of documentation for a single component[f], accessible in different ways, would help these different processes[21].

It would thus seem that justification for decisions taken during the design of the source would be useful during analysis and design while documentation of implementation details would be more useful for reuse during the implemen-tation phase. One limitation of this approach[22], particularly with regard to design rationale, is the difficulty of predicting all the questions about the justification of the design that designers reusing a component in the future might raise. It has been observed[23] that many questions raised during reuse are not answered in the documentation because the culture of the designers has evolved between the production of the component and its reuse. Furthermore, writing documents formalizing the design rationale requires more from designers than the simple capture of knowledge; rather, it needs abstract reflection on their own design activity[24].

4.4 Future Research

The study of reuse in program design has enriched the analogical reasoning models developed in cognitive psychology. One cognitive mechanism that had not previ-ously been analysed is the process of generating an instance of a schema, which is a special case of generation from a source. We have seen that generating an instance, which has the status of a source in analogical reasoning, is accompanied by a very special look-ahead process. This process enriches Clement's model. It would be useful to go further and analyse reuse situations in other application domains in order to confirm this phenomenon and analyse it in more detail.

Another dimension that it seems useful to take into account and which is linked to the nature of the design situation is the design phase in which the analogy is used – analysis, problem solving or coding. This dimension is completely original so far as the literature on reasoning by analogy is concerned. However, this dimen-sion seems, to be a determining factor in choosing the mode of reasoning to be employed, contrasting mechanisms that allow the representation of the target situ-ation to be enriched with those that allow the level of control to be lowered.

---

[f]The use of 'free annotations' (Green, Gilmore, Blumenthal, Davies and Winder, 1992) might be one way of implementing this approach.

Moreover, it would be useful to go further with this classification of reuse situations by taking account of the nature of the problem solving activities in which the analogical reasoning occurs.

References

1. Burkhardt and Détienne, 1995a; Guindon, 1990b; Visser and Hoc, 1990; Visser and Trousse, 1993.
2. McIlroy, 1969.
3. Gentner, 1983, 1989.
4. Holyak, 1985.
5. Vosniadou and Ortony, 1989.
6. Gick and Holyoak, 1983.
7. Clement, 1981, 1986, 1988.
8. Burkhardt and Détienne, 1995b; Rosson and Carroll, 1993; Rouet, Deleuze-Dordron and Bisseret, 1995b.
9. Burkhardt and Détienne, 1995b.
10. Détienne, 1991.
11. Norman and Bobrow, 1979.
12. De Vries, 1993.
13. Burkhardt and Détienne, 1995a, 1995b.
14. Fischer and Nieper-Lemke, 1989; Fischer, Henninger and Redmiles, 1991.
15. Woodfield, Embley and Scott, 1987.
16. Rouet, Deleuze-Dordron and Bisseret, 1995b.
17. Burkhardt and Détienne, 1995a, 1995b; De Vries, 1993.
18. Rosson and Carroll, 1993.
19. Burkhardt and Détienne, 1994.
20. Lange and Moher, 1989; Rosson and Carroll, 1993.
21. Détienne, Rouet, Burkhardt and Deleuze-Dordron, 1996.
22. Moran and Carroll, 1996.
23. Karsenty, 1996.
24. Sauvagnac, Falzon and Leblond, 1997.

5. *Design and Reuse of Object-Oriented Software: the Effect of a Programming Paradigm*

■ ■

In this chapter we shall take up again the points raised in Chapters 3 and 4, in order to illustrate the effect of a programming paradigm, in this case object-orientation (OO[a]), on the design and reuse activities. In the past few years, many studies have produced experimental results concerning design and reuse in an object-oriented environment. We shall present a critical summary of this work.

■ ■

5.1 Cognitive Implications of OO: Hypotheses

One interesting question in the psychology of programming is the impact of a programming paradigm and, more generally, a language type on the activity of programming. In this regard, OO is remarkable for the extent to which its proponents have made strong claims for the cognitive implications of the approach.

5.1.1 The Object-Oriented Approach

The OO paradigm is based on the notions of class, inheritance and encapsulation. In contrast to classical programming techniques, which separate data and procedures, OO suppresses this distinction, by bringing data and processing functions (called methods) together into entities called classes. A class is defined by a data structure and a set of methods used to manipulate objects that are instances of the class. Thus a method is a function attached to a class and it describes part of the behaviour of objects of that class. An object encapsulates a value of the data structure defined by the class.

Classes are organized in the form of a tree. The relations between classes can be of two types : the 'is-a' relation, which defines a specialization between a class and its parent class, and the relation 'is-part-of', which defines a composition link between classes. By the inheritance property, every class inherits the structure and methods of its parent class (under the is-a relation).

---

[a]For convenience, we use the abbreviation both as a noun (object-orientation) and as an adjective (object-oriented).

In OO, abstraction is achieved by means of encapsulation, polymorphism and late binding. Encapsulation means that an object owns its data and methods. Their internal structure is private. They are accessible to, and can be used by, other objects only if these objects send a suitable message to the owner.

Message passing constitutes one of the ways of activating a function attached to a given object. The behaviour of an object is determined by its own interpretation of the message received. This is the property of polymorphism. The same message sent to objects of different classes can cause different methods to be executed. When the program is executed, the method that is called depends on the class of the object which receives the message; this is the principle of late binding.

Plans and objects are orthogonal in OO systems[1]. This reflects the real world in which a plan or a procedure can use several objects (the plan for making a cake uses flour, eggs, butter, etc.) while an object can be used in several different plans (an egg can be used to make a cake, an omelette, a soufflé, etc.) We recall that a plan is a set of programming elements that allow a certain goal to be achieved. In an OO system, elements of a plan are often parts of different methods. These methods can be attached to different classes and linked among themselves by the flow of control (i.e. message passing). Thus plans can be widely dispersed in an OO system.

5.1.2 The Naturalness of OO Design

Designing a program means setting up a mapping between the problem domain and the programming domain. Proponents of OO claim that this mapping is easier with the OO paradigm than with the classical procedural approach. The under-lying theoretical argument is that the objects are entities clearly identified in the problem domain.

The identification of objects (or of classes, since objects are instances of classes) ought to be easy since the objects form natural representations of the problem enti-ties. According to Meyer (1988) the world is naturally structured into objects. It therefore seems particularly appropriate to organize solutions to design problems around the programming representations of these objects. The mapping between the problem domain and the solution domain ought to be simple. The objects of the problem domain are identified and then used to structure the OO system. Thus both the problem and the solution are decomposed on the basis of objects.

With an object-oriented language, problem analysis consists of identifying the objects, the relations between the objects, and the association between the struc-ture (the declarative aspect) and the functions (the procedural aspect) of the objects. We assume that the analysis into objects is natural. This allows us to construct a solution structure. It will be guided by knowledge of the world rather than by knowledge of the design process or programming knowledge[2]. With a procedural language, in contrast, the construction of the solution structure is guided by the generic programming knowledge (e.g. programming schemas). In terms of the concepts of problem space and solution space, this means that there is little overlap between reasoning in the problem space and reasoning in the solu-tion space: objects are considered but remain implicit in the solution space.

From a psychological point of view, one may wonder whether the objects are really the basis for constructing the solution structure. This will certainly depend on the type of problem. What is more, it is not clear that the linkage between the declarative aspects and the procedural aspects of the solution is based on the notion of object. Some authors[3] claim that knowledge is organized on the basis of goals and procedures rather than on relational knowledge about objects. Procedures are properties of objects and constitute the basis for classifying objects. Relational knowledge comes second and is constructed to justify the procedures. According to this approach, one might expect that the development of the procedural aspects of the solution would determine the relations between the objects. This is a point of view completely at variance with the hypothesis that OO is, in some sense, natural.

It is worth remarking that early books on OO emphasized how easy it was to identify objects while later ones, often by the same authors, emphasize the difficulty of identifying them.

5.1.3 Better Reusability of OO Components

The property of encapsulation in OO programming ought to facilitate and encourage the reuse of software components: the code is encapsulated in the objects and the internal details of each object remain hidden. However, encapsulation is not the prerogative of OO programming languages. The hypothesis concerning the better reusability of OO components rests rather on the idea that the hierarchies that form the class model are particularly well adapted to reuse. The programmer need only select a hierarchy of objects appropriate to the problem domain and then specialize it in an appropriate manner by adding subclasses suitable for a particular problem. In this way, the structure and functions offered by the parent classes are automatically available through inheritance. This means that one tries to lift attributes as high as possible in the hierarchy, towards the most abstract classes.

This principle, however, is directly contrary to categorization behaviour as described in cognitive psychology on the basis of empirical studies. It has been shown[4] that in category hierarchies certain objects have a special cognitive status. They are called basic level objects; they stand at an intermediate level of abstraction and form an anchor point for classification and reasoning[b]. Such objects have a large number of discriminating attributes while higher categories in the 'natural' hierarchies have many less. Thus the highest categories have few attributes to bequeath to the lower categories, which is inimical to the idea of reuse by inheritance in OO. From this point of view, therefore, the hypothesis regarding the greater reusability of OO components must be questioned.

5.2 Object-Oriented Design

Empirical studies of object-oriented design[5], carried out in recent years, have produced many individual results that help to evaluate the hypothesis that the

---

[b]For example, in the hierarchy living thing, animal, mammal, bear, polar bear, it is bear that is the basic level object for a large majority of humans.

object-oriented approach can be considered 'natural'. We present here a summary of these results.

5.2.1 Mapping Between the Problem Space and the Solution Space

There have been a number of comparative studies[6] that address this issue. It has been shown that OO design tends to be faster and easier than procedural design. According to the hypothesis that OO is a natural approach to design, the analysis of the problem and the construction of a solution structure should be guided by the entities in the problem domain and this has been confirmed by several of the studies, which have also shown that in procedural programming it is guided by generic knowledge or knowledge schemas.

It has been shown that OO experts analyse the problem through its objects. Compared to procedural design, the analysis of the problem situation takes less time in OO and the description of the objects and their relationships takes more. OO designers define the classes by using their knowledge of the objects in the problem domain and of how they interact. On the basis of these observations, it has been suggested that OO design, in its initial phases, is based on understanding of the problem itself rather than on specialized knowledge of design, i.e. programming schemas. In contrast, procedural design solutions are structured by generic knowledge of programming rather than problem domain entities.

Solutions produced by different designers are more similar when the designers are working within the OO framework than when they are working within a procedural framework. This similarity may be attributed to the fact that the structure of the solution is based on knowledge of the problem, something that is shared by all the subjects. Thus OO designers tend to create solutions that have a fairly close correspondence with the problem domain.

A design method that will lead to lead any designer using it to produce essentially the same (correct!) design has long been the philosopher's stone of software engineering research. Not only would such a method reduce the number of design errors in software systems, it would also make it easier for people other than the designer to understand the design. This property of OO design methods, if it can be verified on a large scale, is an important step in that direction.

5.2.2 OO Programming Schemas

In considering the knowledge-based approach to design we distinguished two types of schema depending on whether they were rich in content or simply structural; the former were called knowledge schemas or programming schemas and the latter, structural schemas. The term kernel is used to refer to programming schemas, both in OO and in procedural design, that allow an abstract solution plan to be formulated very early in the design.

An experiment[7] allowed expertise in OO programming to be taken into account in a program segmentation task and in a program design task. Program segmentation is used particularly for identifying the different categories of schema that experts possess. In OO, the following types of schema were identified: application domain schemas, function schemas, procedure schemas and object schemas. While the first three of these types are knowledge schemas and rich in content, the fourth type is a structural schema.

An application domain schema describes the objects and the functions belonging to the problem posed.

A function schema is an elementary programming schema; it represents a sequence of actions implementing a function typical of the object. A procedure schema is a complex programming schema; it represents the objects and the functions that have to be manipulated to achieve some given goal. These two categories of schema are very similar to the elementary schemas and complex schemas described in Section 3.1 to account for the knowledge of experts in procedural programming. One difference relates to the explicit character of the objects and the links to objects in the schemas relating to OO programming.

An object schema represents structural characteristics of an object, i.e. the data or attributes, and generic characteristics of the functions associated with it, i.e. their roles. Thus, for example, the object schema for any object to be displayed must include a 'print' or 'display' method. Recall that, according to the structural or story grammar approach, a text of a certain type can be described according to a structure appropriate to this kind of text. For OO programmes, for example in Smalltalk, these structural object schemas associate with a generic object a certain number of roles: creation, initialization, read access, write access, input, output.

It has also been observed that 'real' OO novices, with no previous experience of procedural programming, begin decomposing their solution by creating classes to which are associated typical functions or roles, which reflects the implementation of structural schemas. It appears therefore that these structural schemas are acquired very early in the learning of an OO language, well before the acquisition of complex programming schemas. This is similar to what has been found in procedural programming[8].

5.2.3 Design Strategies

As with procedural programming, we can separate the strategies used in OO programming according to whether they are data-driven (or declarative) or process-driven (or procedural) and we can show how expertise, environment and problem type affect the way the strategies are used.

When the strategy is declarative, static characteristics, such as objects and typical functions or roles, guide the development of the solution. Such strategies may be function-centred or object-centred:

- function-centred strategies: functions are central to the representation that guides the design activity and objects are subordinate to functions. Designers develop a typical function for several objects, then another typical function for several objects, etc. Examples of such functions are: read access, write access, initialization, printing, etc.;

- object-centred strategies: objects are central to the representation that guides the design process. Functions and procedures are subordinate to objects. Designers thus develop several typical functions for one object then for another object, and so on.

When the strategy is procedural, dynamic characteristics, such as the temporal ordering of the execution of the actions of a procedure, control the development of the solution. In OO programming such a procedure is a complex plan which is distributed, in the sense that the different actions of the plan correspond to different methods that are associated with different objects. Client-server relationships, such as call structure, provide links between these actions. When they follow a procedure-centred strategy, designers develop a chain of several methods involved in a procedure, following their call links, even if the methods are associated with different objects.

Just as with procedural programming, mental simulation is an important strategy.

Again, an important research question is to determine the conditions that trigger each of these strategies. Expertise, programming environment, and problem type all play a part. For sufficiently complex problems, programmers probably use a combination of several strategies.

Effect of Expertise

So far as the effect of expertise on the strategy chosen is concerned, the results of studies are contradictory. In Détienne (1995) a procedure-centred strategy was most used by beginners, while the object-centred strategy was found to be typical of the experts; in Rist (1996), the procedure-centred strategy was most used by experienced subjects; and it was used by experts handling problems of procedural type in Chatel and Détienne (1996). One explanation of these contradictory results may be the way in which the different studies clarify subjects as 'experts'. The expert subjects in Rist's study are, in fact, advanced students, while they are professionals in the others. This would explain why experienced programmes in Rist's study behave like novices in Détienne's.

Although these studies show that each group of subjects has a dominant strategy, they also show that programmers use a variety of strategies in the course of their design activity. Rist discusses this phenomenon and concludes that design is an activity controlled locally by various factors and organized in an opportunistic way.

Effect of the Programming Environment

So far as the effect of the programming environment is concerned, it is clear that certain of its features can encourage one strategy rather than another. For example, one difference between the studies mentioned above by Détienne (1995) and Chatel and Détienne (1996) lies in the language and programming environment used by the subjects, CO2 in the first study and Smalltalk in the second. It is probable that one feature of the Smalltalk environment encouraged the use of a function-centred strategy. The methods that implement the same function for different objects, e.g. initialization, can be regrouped by the designer into a single category of methods under the same label. That may encourage the designer to treat all the methods implementing the same function as a bunch.

Effect of the Problem Type

As we remarked in Section 3.3, the classification of problems into declarative or procedural, depending on whether the complexity lies in the data structure or the procedures, has been challenged in the context of OO design. A new dimension has been introduced that characterises not only the structure of the objects (or data) on the one hand, and the structure of the procedure on the other, but also the way in which the two are connected. The strategy used by experts in OO is declarative when the problem exhibits a hierarchical solution structure with vertical communication between the objects, while the strategy is procedural when the problem exhibits a flat solution structure with horizontal communication between the objects.

5.2.4 Organization of the Design Process

Opportunistic vs Hierarchical Organization

In Section 3.5.2 we noted that empirical studies have demonstrated the opportunistic nature of the design process in the procedural paradigm. This is also true in OO programming. One research question has been to compare the OO approach with the procedural approach, to see whether it leads to more opportunistic deviations or fewer. On this point, two comparative studies have produced contradictory results.

One study[9] found that experts in procedural programming make more opportunistic deviations while experts in OO stick more closely to top-down, breadth first development. In contrast, another study[10] has observed the opposite.

It appears that these different results may derive from the different experimental conditions of the two studies. The first study was done with paper and pencil, that is, the designers had no programming environment available for their use, while the subjects in the second study did. We may therefore wonder whether it was the effect of the paradigm or the effect of the environment that was being measured.

It seems that certain OO programming environments encourage opportunistic design; one such is the Smalltalk environment[11]. But we would not support the view that any object-oriented environment encourages opportunism. For example, the CO2 environment, at least in one of the first versions we evaluated, constrained designers to follow a hierarchical development process: classes had to be created in a top-down fashion and every method had to be defined in a class before being used in the code. We described this feature in terms of cognitive dimensions in Section 4.2.1: the environment has features that result in premature commitment. Clearly these features are not dependent on the OO character of the environment.

Connection Between the Declarative and Procedural Aspects of the Solution

Certain methods of OO design as well as certain environments, such as CO2, impose a hierarchical approach: roughly speaking, it is necessary to define the declarative aspects of the solution, i.e. classes and their relationships, before the procedural aspects, that is the code of the methods. It has been shown that beginners tend to follow the methods they learned on their course: they identify the objects in the problem domain, then the classes, then the methods. They hope that the classes thus created will be useful later. Novices – and even experts in certain conditions – face two main types of related difficulty: the difficulty of identifying the classes and the difficulty of connecting the declarative and procedural aspects of the solution.

Even if the novices begin by identifying the objects and the classes, as laid down by OO design methods, this identification is not without difficulties[12]. Novices spend a considerable time identifying and rejecting problem domain objects as potential classes for their solution. They postpone the treatment of goals. In fact, many classes that are created in a first design phase will reveal themselves as useless later, while other classes not anticipated in this early phase will be found to be essential.

The declarative and procedural aspects of the solution are not brought together until late in the design. More often than experts, novices describe the objects and the actions or procedures separately in their first versions of the solution. Associating the declarative and procedural aspects often means decomposing a large procedure, developed to handle one of the problem goals, into smaller functional units. Rather than decompose the procedure, novices sometimes associate the whole thing with a single class, although this is obviously not in accordance with OO orthodoxy.

When they come to write the code of the methods, novices refine certain aspects of the classes previously defined at a more abstract level; they might add attributes for example. Many revisions of the class model are observed when the subjects develop the procedural aspect of the solution – addition, deletion and reorganization of classes, adding methods, changing the assignment of methods to classes. We note that these changes to the methods concern the definition of a complex plan and the linking of the actions of the plan to the objects.

5.2.5 Development of Expertise in OO

Two aspects of the development of expertise in OO are particularly interesting: the effects of the transfer of knowledge acquired from other paradigms and misconceptions acquired while learning OO ideas.

Negative Effects of the Transfer of Knowledge

The effects of changing from one programming language to another have been widely studied[13]. Learning an n'th language seems to pose many problems concerning the learning of new solution schemas but few problems relating to the acquisition of new syntactic and semantic knowledge. Known schemas are transferred and have negative effects on design in the new language. These schemas are often unsuited to the new language but subjects have a tendency to use them, making only local changes if at all possible[c]. If this proves impossible, more profound revisions are undertaken. This has been found to be true even when the new programming language belongs to the same language paradigm as the old one.

---

[c]Somewhat similar phenomena are apparent when we are talking about acquisition of a new natural language.

It is natural to ask whether this effect is more or less important when passing from a procedural language to an OO language. Proponents of object-oriented programming hold that, when learning it, existing knowledge of the application domain should help to analyse the problem and to decompose and structure the solution. However, most beginners in OO are programmers experienced in other programming paradigms, usually procedural programming, and the knowledge transferred appertains not only to the application domain but also to other programming languages and approaches to design.

One example of the negative effects of such transfer relates to a novice who was using attributes of type *integer* in each class, in order to link together objects, instead of using the composition relation 'is-part-of'. Through talking to the subject, it became apparent that he had constructed his solution by using data analysis methods typically employed when using a relational database management system as the implementation environment. In this approach, integers are associated with different objects and serve as indexes to link them together and facilitate database searches. The subject had thus used a very flat class structure instead of using the composition relation between objects. Such a solution does not conform to OO principles.

Another example of the negative effects of transfer from another language is provided by the novice who added a parameter 'object-type' to a class. This was to allow him to carry out different processing according to the value taken by this parameter, which would be used to control a **case** statement. Such a solution is typical of a procedural approach and does not exploit the functionality of OO languages. Late binding and inheritance make it possible for the system itself to handle these matters and thus avoid the need both for the 'object-type' parameter and the **case** statement.

It is an open question whether or how these transfer effects differ when the OO language is one that resembles a procedural language already known to the learner. It is possible that the similarity might facilitate both the transfer of schemas and the interference between the two. C++ and CO2 both have procedural features, due to their similarity to C, that are not present on other OO languages such as Smalltalk. Most studies of these languages demonstrate the existence of transfers and of their negative effects. However, the existence of transfers has also been demonstrated during the learning of languages such as Smalltalk.

Acquisition of Concepts

Studies of beginners in OO have demonstrated their lack of understanding of certain OO concepts, in particular the concepts of class and inheritance. Beginners tend to think of a class as a set of objects and thus attribute various properties of sets to the concept of class. This misconception is revealed by some of the errors they make. For example, to define a function that processes a set of objects of class X, they associate this function with the class X instead of creating a class Y that would represent a set of objects of class X and then associating the function with class Y.

Novices also have a tendency to believe that instances of a class are created by default. Thus they tend to use instances of a class without previously creating them.

This type of error is similar to forgetting to initialize variables in a procedural program. Initializing a variable or creating an object are not necessary prerequisites in a real world situation and do not therefore form part of the knowledge that is transferred from the real world. In general, if we leave aside transfer of knowledge from procedural programming, novices learn by analogy with the problem situation in the application domain. The problem situation in the application domain is the source situation, while the problem situation in OO is the target situation. In this case, there are preconditions on the target situation that are automatically satisfied in the source situation.

Beginners also have erroneous ideas about inheritance. They try to use it as often as possible, very often in an inappropriate fashion. On the one hand, they tend to treat the abstraction hierarchy as a composition hierarchy. On the other hand, they have more difficulty using inheritance for functional properties, i.e. the methods of a class, than for its static properties, such as its attributes.

5.2.6 Cognitive Implications of OO: Naturalness

How far can we assess the hypothesis that OO is 'natural'? Experiments using beginners in OO show that they have difficulties in creating suitable classes and in linking the declarative and procedural aspects of their solutions. These results therefore undermine the hypothesis put forward by the proponents of OO. First, they show that the identification of objects is not an easy process. Entities are identified as objects on the basis of knowledge about the problem but these entities do not necessarily prove useful in the design solution. The mapping between the problem domain and the computing domain is not direct. The analysis of the problem domain is not enough to structure the solution in terms of objects. Beginners need to construct a representation of the procedural aspects of the solution in order to refine, evaluate and revise their decomposition into classes with associated objects.

These results suggest that a representation of certain procedural aspects of the solution is built up before the representation of the more declarative aspects, e.g., the objects. This contradicts the hypothesis about the naturalness of OO. On the other hand, it accords with the hypotheses of cognitive ergonomics, that:

- knowledge is organized starting from goals and procedures and not from relational knowledge about objects or other declarative aspects;
- procedures are properties of objects and they form the basis for classifying objects[14].

Studies of experts in OO apparently confirm the hypothesis about the naturalness of OO. They show that the decomposition of the problem is guided by the problem entities, while in procedural programming it is guided by schematic programming knowledge. OO experts spend as much time as experts in procedural programming in analysing the problem domain but they do it through the creation of classes rather than in general terms. This suggest that OO designers analyse the situation through objects and their relations.

The result of putting these ideas together seems rather paradoxical. If decomposition is guided by knowledge of the problem domain, the greatest benefit should be felt by novices. But this is not what is observed. We offer two explanations. First, the novices used as subjects were not novice programmers but only novices in OO; it is possible, therefore, that the results obtained mainly reflect the negative effects of transfer of knowledge developed for use in other paradigms. From this point of view, it would be very valuable to collect data on real novices, with no previous knowledge of programming.

A second explanation is based on the nature of the knowledge built up through experience of OO. It has been suggested that schemas are constructed during the process of gaining experience with the OO paradigm and that these guide OO design. Procedure schemas regroup the actions of a procedure according to their order of execution. Function schemas represent typical basic functions, such as initialization or read access. Object schemas bring together actions and objects, with actions organized around objects. They can be more or less structural, more or less rich in content. It is these schemas that are built up through experience with OO, and which beginners in OO lack.

Further, experimental results show that experts in OO change design strategies and can thus pass from an object-centred strategy to a procedure-centred strategy when developing their solutions. This shows that both the object-centred view and the procedure-centred view are important. This suggests[15] that objects and plans are orthogonal and that both types of entity are conceptually equally important. They are two valid and important views of OO systems that can be used to guide the design process.

5.2.7 Practical Implications

Programming environments can facilitate the deployment of the different strategies that have been observed in empirical studies: procedure-centred, function-centred or object-centred. Different ways of visualizing programs that can be found in current commercially available environments include:

- a representation of the message call graph, to support a procedure-centred strategy;
- a representation of the organization of the classes and roles, to support object-centred and function-centred strategies.

The environment might also be aware of some of the conditions that control which type of strategy is adopted. For example, if the user develops a flat class hierarchy, we have seen that the strategy is likely to be procedure-centred. In such a case the environment might offer the call graph representation as the default visualization mode.

Typically, tools that display the inheritance graph display only classes and it is not possible to get a global picture of the classes with their associated methods. Such a tool would be valuable.

We have seen that designers encounter two types of difficulty in object-oriented design: linking the declarative and procedural aspects of the solution and visualizing complex plans (or distributed procedures). It seems difficult at present to specify tools to support the linking process. More generally, however, it is probable that displays of the static structure, the dynamic structure, and their links could be useful to the designer: such tools have been developed for visualizing Smalltalk programs[16]. Complex plans could then be displayed through client-server relations and, in particular, the method call graph.

Some tutorial tools have already been developed[17] to make the transfer between procedural languages easier and especially to control the negative effects of interference from one language into another. These tools use artificial intelligence techniques that allow the plans developed by the student to be compared with a knowledge base of correct plans in the target language and alternative plans to be suggested. So far as we are aware no such tools exist to facilitate transfer between languages belonging to different paradigms.

On this point, some recommendations have been made[18] for detecting, and warning of, negative transfer effects during training in a new, OO language. The training should be based on the programmers' previous knowledge. Thus, for the same problem or sub-problem, the classical procedural solution and an OO solution might be presented together, while taking care to explain the difference in the way the two solutions work. It would also be important to identify the analogies that the programmers make in order to understand the new concepts in object-oriented programming. For example, the procedure call structure serves as a reference point for understanding message passing. The training might take up and develop this analogy by explaining on which points the two structures differ.

5.3 Reuse in the OO Paradigm

Just as the hypothesis of the naturalness of OO design can be tested against recent empirical studies, such studies also help to evaluate the hypothesis of the better reusability of object-oriented components. Again, we present a summary of these results.

5.3.1 Reuse in a Procedural Paradigm vs Reuse in OO

So far as we are aware there has only been one study of how reuse using a procedural programming language compares with reuse using OO. This exploratory study[19] demonstrated a gain in productivity using OO, which the investigators attributed in large part to the reuse mechanisms in that paradigm. Their conclusions were the following:

- the OO paradigm leads to an increase in productivity, although this increase is due in large part to the effects of reuse;
- reuse increases productivity whatever the programming paradigm;
- differences between languages are much more important when reuse is practised than when it is not;
- the OO paradigm has a special affinity for the reuse process.

Some studies on the modifiability of OO programs also provide results about their reusability, given that modification often forms part of the reuse process. One study of the maintenance of OO systems[20] shows that programmers experienced in structured design but with little experience of OO design encounter serious problems in understanding and maintaining OO systems. In contrast, another study[21] has found that, for students, OO programs are more easily modifiable than procedural programs. Another study[22] has found the opposite result, for students, when the modifications to be done are complex. For professionals, the programming paradigm was found to have no effect on modifiability. However, in this last study, the object-oriented programs were written using an object-oriented version of Pascal that did not have all the features usually associated with OO programming; in particular, it lacked inheritance.

5.3.2 Potential Reuse in OO

One way of evaluating the reuse potential of OO is to analyse the consistency of the solutions and representations constructed by different designers. It has been observed[23] that, for the same problem tackled by different designers, there are more similarities between the OO solutions than between the procedural solutions produced. The OO solutions include similar objects and methods, while the procedural solutions are distinguished by the data structures and procedural decompositions chosen.

This consistency can be linked to knowledge in the application or problem domain shared by the designers. A study[24] of the construction of a class hierarchy demonstrated that differences in knowledge of the application domain affect the inter-subject agreement on the structure of the class hierarchies produced. The consistency decreases as the hierarchy becomes deeper. A study[25] in which designers had to build a hierarchy on the basis of class specifications shows that, the deeper the hierarchy constructed, the less the subjects are in agreement on the placement of a class within the hierarchy. The concept of 'conceptual entropy' is used to explain this result. Conceptual entropy shows itself in the form of an increase in conceptual inconsistencies as one goes down the hierarchy. The lower the level in the hierarchy, the greater the probability that a sub-class will not be specialized in a fashion consistent with the concepts of its parent classes. This concept may explain the results of a recent study[26] in which the performance of the subjects in a maintenance task was worse with a five level hierarchy than with a three level one.

Reuse by inheritance is a mode of reuse that is based on the organization of objects into a hierarchical structure. Thus reuse in OO is based on the hypothesis that the representation of the objects is the most important and that it corresponds to the deep structure of the program. A number of studies[27] have called parts of this hypothesis into question:

- experts may reason about OO programs in three different ways: a procedural view, a function-centred view, and an object-centred view;
- functional properties and message passing relations, which denote the procedural view, are more important to experts than to novices. Experts tend to base their reasoning on the algorithmic structure;
- relations between objects are more important for novices than for experts. Novices tend to base their reasoning on the problem domain, even if this proves a source of errors.

These results challenge the idea that objects form the deep structure of of OO programs. In general, it is probable that different tasks entail different perspectives on the code, and not just a point of view centred on objects.

5.3.3 Cognitive Mechanisms Deployed in OO Reuse

One preliminary remark concerns the two forms of reuse in OO programming, reuse by inheritance and reuse of code. While the first form is the one that is preached in the cathedrals of object-oriented orthodoxy, some studies[28] demonstrate that frequent recourse is made to code reuse, by simple duplication or by copying and modifying it. We shall describe certain of the cognitive mechanisms that seem to us to be used in reuse by inheritance, concentrating on the processes of understanding and reusing a source. There are two mechanisms that may be used for generating a source:

1. finding a source in an existing hierarchy;

2. creating a source with a view to reusing it.

There have been no studies, to our knowledge, of the first of these mechanisms. So far as the second is concerned, the 'new code reuse' situation, described in Section 4.3.1, demonstrates the creation of a source; the source is the first instance of a schema and, in the OO context, is the sibling of another sub-class, which will then be specialized.

Understanding the Source

Two ways of understanding the source are proposed in the literature of class reuse in OO: use of the context in which the source class was used, and use of existing familiarity. We shall see that these two modes seem to be triggered by quite different situations.

When designers are not familiar with the source class that they are required to reuse and this source class has been reused in several example applications that they have not developed themselves, studying the contexts in which it has been used will enable them to construct a representation of it that includes the relations that it has with other parts of the program. The effect will be to generate a larger source than the class itself that was identified at the beginning. The reuse situation in Smalltalk described by Rosson and Carrol (1993), which they call 'reuse of uses' is of this type. Designers were invited to modify object-oriented programs by reusing existing classes; it was observed that they frequently had recourse to an example application that used the source class. That allowed them to understand the source class itself and also to understand its links with other classes in the example program. Two methods were used to determine precisely the context in which the source was being used: simulation of a part or the whole of the example program and the use of a Smalltalk feature called 'sender query' that displays a list of methods in which a message (in this case a message from the source class) is handled.

This understanding focused on the use of the source class in a program not analogous to the target program has the following effects. It allows a source to be generated that is broader than the source class originally considered. The designer might, for example, decide to reuse the class plus some of the other features linked to it. Furthermore, the example application provides designers with implicit specifications for using the source class, particularly a lot of contextual information.

In certain cases, designers reuse the whole of the context of the source class by deciding reuse the class by inheritance. This idea has been developed in software engineering under the name of 'framework'[29].

In contrast to what has been described above, it may happen that the designer has developed the source class himself in the more or less recent pass and that it forms part of the same program as the target class. The designer is therefore relatively familiar with the relations between the source class and the other parts of the program. In this case, the effort necessary to understand the source is minimal.

Use of the Source

In reuse by inheritance, a particular mechanism of specialization from the parent class must be used to define a sub-class. In this example of reasoning by analogy, in which the parent class takes the role of the source and the sub-class the role of target, new methods or structures have to be defined and added to the source or existing ones have to be modified. In the 'new code reuse' scenario described earlier, these mechanisms are borne in mind when the source itself, which is a first specialization of the parent class (and of a schema), is generated. In contrast, when the class has already been constructed, which is often the case, it appears that two types of cognitive mechanism are employed when using the source: using a class placed in the position of a sibling to the target class as a bridging case (see Section 4.1.2), and a trial and error strategy.

Lange and Moher (1989) have demonstrated the special role of the class that is a sibling to the one that has to be created or modified during a reuse episode in OO. This class is used very frequently and serves as a template for creating the target. We regard the parent class as playing the role of the source for the analogical reasoning; it is the source that is modified in order to create the target class by specialization. The sibling class represents an analogous situation intermediate between the source class (here the parent class) and the target class. The sibling class is used as a tool to help reuse the parent class. It serves as a model for modifying it. The parent class is specialized to create the target class in a way similar to that in which the it was specialized to produce the sibling class. While in Clement's model, the bridging analogy is used only in the course of the second process (establishing confidence in the analogical relationship), in the situation described by Lange and Moher it seems rather that this type of analogy is being used in the final process, that is, applying the results.

Trial and error strategies when using the source have been observed in the majority of studies concerned with reuse in OO. Subjects make modifications to adapt the source to their needs and then immediately use debugging tools to check whether the modifications are correct. This strategy is very often accompanied by comprehension avoidance but it may also be used when the subject has recourse to an example programme to understand the source. Rather than understand the code in detail, designers make the modifications that seem the most plausible and test them immediately. Testing is used regularly by designers when using sources, even when they know for certain that the target program thus generated is wrong.

5.3.4 Cognitive Implications of OO: Summary of Experimental Findings on Reuse

Some results of empirical studies confirm the idea that the OO paradigm encourages reuse. They show, in particular, that the OO paradigm improves productivity and that a non-negligible part of this gain in productivity is due to the effects of reuse. The potential for reuse in OO is also attested by the greater consistency between the solutions produced by different designers using OO, in comparison with designers using a procedural paradigm. This consistency seems to be due to shared knowledge of the problem domain.

The form of reuse encouraged by OO programming is reuse by inheritance. There are, however, two types of results that call into question the ease with which such an approach can be applied. First, while reuse by inheritance is based on the concept of an object, some studies challenge the idea that objects constitute the deep structure of object-oriented programs. Two other views – the procedural view and the functional view – seem equally important.

Second, empirical studies show that use of the inheritance properties is often eschewed in favour of code duplication. The problem with code duplication is that it decentralizes and duplicates functionality, which makes it difficult to propagate modifications and corrections subsequently made to the source. Further, reuse of classes via inheritance is far from being something that beginners do spontaneously. These results suggest that reuse may require a special expertise and, in this regard, questions about training in reuse and documentation for reuse seem particularly important.

5.3.5 Practical Implications

Over and above the implications discussed in Chapter 4, the work described above demonstrates the need for help in understanding the context in which a source is used. While this need is not peculiar to OO, at the very least it is reinforced by the situation in OO, where it is difficult to gain an idea a priori of the relations between a source class and the other parts of the program. In an object-oriented program, plans and objects are orthogonal. Thus the actions belonging to a complex procedure or plan are spread through different classes. In reusing a class, it is therefore fundamental to analyse the relations that it may have with other classes in the program. We have shown how the designer can look for this type of information in an example program that uses the source class. It therefore seems fundamental to provide examples of the use of classes that make up a class library.

An experimental reuse documentation tool (the Reuse View Matcher) has been developed for Smalltalk, to help understand the context in which a class is used by an explicit example. This allows an example application of a source class selected by the designer to be animated through the execution of a small set of scenarios. The designer also has access to more detailed information on the use that has been made of the class during the animation.

5.4 Future Research

Studies of reuse in OO design have enriched analogical reasoning models, especially in areas concerned with comprehension mechanisms and mechanisms for using the source.

We have shown that the understanding of a source and, especially, the understanding of a context in which the source is used, e.g. an example program not analogous to the target program, allows the designer

- to generate a broader source: in terms of Clement's model, this involves an iteration between the third stage (understanding the source) and the first stage (generating the source);
- to collect information relating to the use of the source in the target context.

These mechanisms seem completely new and deserve deeper study.

Another completely original mechanism, and one that is dependent the phase of using the source, is the construction of a bridging analogy with a sub-class of the source that is a sibling of the target. The construction of bridging analogies is used in the second stage (establishing confidence in the analogy) of Clement's model. Studies of reuse in OO illustrate the same phenomenon being applied in the fourth phase. Again this phenomenon needs deeper investigation.

References

1. Rist and Terwilliger, 1995.
2. Rosson and Alpert, 1990.
3. Richard, 1996.
4. Rosch, 1978; Rosch, Mervis, Gray, Johnson and Boyes-Braem, 1975.
5. Détienne and Rist, 1995.
6. Kim and Lerch, 1992; Boehm-Davies and Ross, 1992; Lee and Pennington, 1994; Pennington, Lee and Rehder, 1995; Rosson & Gold, 1989.
7. Chatel, 1997; Chatel and Détienne, 1994.
8. Rist, 1989.
9. Lee and Pennington, 1994; Pennington, Lee and Rehder, 1995.
10. Brangier and Bobiller-Chaumon, 1995.
11. Bellamy, 1994b; Rosson and Carroll, 1993.
12. Détienne, 1995; Pennington, Lee and Rehder, 1995.
13. Chatel, Détienne and Borne, 1992; Détienne, 1990a, 1990d, 1995; Pennington, Lee and Rehder, 1995; Siddiqi, Osborne, Roast and Khazaei, 1996; Scholtz and Wiedenbeck, 1990a, 1990b, 1993; Wu and Anderson, 1991.
14. Richard, 1996.
15. Rist, 1996.
16. Böcker and Herczeg, 1990.
17. Fix and Wiedenbeck, 1996.
18. Détienne, 1990d.
19. Lewis, Henry, Kafura and Schulman, 1991.
20. Van Hillegersberg, Kumar and Welke, 1995.
21. Henry and Humphrey, 1993.
22. Boehm-Davis, Holt and Schultz, 1992.
23. Lee and Pennington, 1994; Boehm-Davis and Ross, 1992.
24. Dvorak and Moher, 1991.
25. Dvorak, 1994.
26. Daly, Brooks, Miller, Roper and Wood, 1996.
27. Davies, Gilmore and Green, 1995; Chatel and Détienne, 1994.
28. For example, Lange and Moher, 1989.
29. Fischer, Redmiles, Williams, Puhr, Aoki and Nakakoji, 1995.

6. *Understanding Software*

In this chapter, we shall describe some models of the way that programmers understand software; these models are based on models of the way that readers understand text. As a preliminary, therefore, in Section 6.1 we present a brief survey of the different theoretical approaches to the understanding of natural language text. We shall then present the different theoretical approaches to program understanding. There are two contrasting types of approach: program understanding seen as text understanding, described in Section 6.2, and program understanding seen as problem solving, described in Section 6.3. For the first type of approach, three models have been borrowed from the study of text understanding: functional models originating in the work of Schank, structural models derived from the theoretical work of authors such as Mandler, Johnson, Rumelhart and Kintsch, and models that incorporate the idea of a mental or situational model, associated with the work of van Dijk and Kintsch. We shall describe these three types of model and discuss how the understanding of software has been used to provide experimental validation of these approaches. While the problem solving approach incorporates the functional approach, it puts the emphasis on the importance of selective processes and representations in understanding software. We shall show that the situational model also takes account of these processes. Finally, we shall discuss the practical implications of the work we have described.

6.1 Models of Text Understanding

The concept of text understanding takes us back to the concept of representation and to the concept of processing. The activity of understanding consists of constructing representations, this construction being accomplished by means of information handling processes. The concept of understanding also takes us back to the concept of knowledge: in the course of reading a text, the reader constructs successive representations by means of processes for handling linguistically coded information. These processes rest on acquired knowledge stored in long-term memory. To understand a text is to construct at a specific instant a representation of the text starting from the handling of information extracted from the text and from acquired knowledge. Thus the information processed comes from two sources: an external source, the information coded in the text, and an internal source, knowledge stored in memory.

The processes involved in understanding have two characteristics: they are interpretative and integrative. The representation constructed is an interpretation of the text; it integrates information explicit in the text with information that must be inferred. The knowledge structures invoked allow information missing from the text to be inferred and also allow information to be modified to ensure consistency. It is a feature of the representation constructed that it integrates the information in the text into a coherent whole. This construction and integration are achieved thanks to the various processes that rest on the information explicit in the text and on acquired knowledge.

Extracting explicit information from the text triggers the activation of knowledge. The knowledge structures activated allow information implicit in the text to be inferred. By this process of inference, relationships are constructed among the pieces of information explicit in the text. It is thanks to this process that different pieces of information can be integrated into a single representation. Consider the following example quoted by Rumelhart (1981, p. 1):

> Mary heard the ice cream truck coming down the street. She remembered her birthday money and rushed into the house.

The majority of readers will form an interpretation of this text that brings together the different events in this story along the following lines: Mary is a little girl who wants to buy an ice cream and, to this end, goes to look for her money in the house. This interpretation integrates the pieces of information that are explicit in the text with information inferred on the basis of the readers' pragmatic knowledge.

As we have already noted, three different types of model have been developed to explain the process of understanding texts written in natural language: the functional (or 'function content') approach, the structural approach, and the mental model approach. These models are distinguished according to:

- the direction in which the information is processed, whether it is top-down or bottom-up;
- the type of knowledge employed, whether it is structural or content-rich;
- the type of representation constructed.

6.1.1 Functional Models

According to the functional approach[1], the processes of understanding are mostly top-down. The reader invokes content schemas, that is schemas that are rich in content, generally called knowledge schemas, for example, scenarios or scripts. These activation processes allow the reader to make inferences and create expectations regarding the information contained in the text. The representations constructed are conceptual.

According to the functional approach, understanding corresponds to the application of knowledge schemas. This model has been developed to account for the understanding of narrative texts.

6.1.2 Structural Models

Two types of model can claim to exemplify the structural approach: the structured schema approach, which derives from work on story grammars, and the propositional network approach. According to these approaches, understanding means constructing a network of relations.

The structured schema approach[2] shares the top-down orientation with the functional approach. This model is strictly structural, however. Structural schemas are activated in the course of reading texts and they guide the processes of understanding. Structural schemas, or *superstructures*, invoked in the course of these top-down processes, represent the generic structure of stories (for example, a story is made up of a framework, a goal, attempts at resolution, actual resolution) rather than the content of the entities (for example, the type of the goal or the type of the resolution). The representation constructed is propositional. It is made up of propositions (a proposition is made up of a predicate and one or more arguments) that are connected among themselves by structural links.

The propositional network approach[3] is also structural but differs from the preceding approach in that the orientation of the understanding processes is mainly bottom-up. The representation constructed is still propositional but the propositions are linked among themselves by referential links. Real world knowledge is not used in constructing these propositional networks. According to this approach, understanding depends in large part on identifying the referential coherence among the textual elements. The referential coherence corresponds to the sharing of arguments among the propositions in the text.

In a more recent development of the model[4], the two preceding approaches have been brought together in a way that involves both bottom-up processes, for constructing propositions, and top-down processes, for applying structural schemas. Three stages are identified in the construction of the propositional representation. The first stage consists of morpho-syntactic decoding, that is, identifying morphemes (words and meaningful parts of words). The second stage consists, first, of carrying out a syntactic analysis of the morpheme string obtained in the first stage, that is, parsing each sentence. Propositions are then constructed on the basis of a lexical analysis and the syntactic structure of the grammatical clauses.

The third stage consists of setting up relations between the propositions and, in particular, arranging them in a hierarchy. There are two phases:

- building the microstructure of the text, that is, arranging the propositions that correspond to the local level of discourse into a coherent hierarchy. The coherence is based on argument overlap;
- building the macrostructure of the text, starting from the microstructure and macrorules,or rules for reducing the semantic information: rules of generalization, suppression, integration and construction.

It is supposed that superstructures can influence the construction of the propositional representation, especially during the building of the macrostructure. A superstructure, such as has been analysed in researches on story grammars, is a structural schema that provides the global syntax of the text, for example,the plan of a scientific article (research framework, hypotheses, method, findings, discussion, concluding remarks). Thus, if a text is organized in a conventional manner, invocation of superstructure can help to guide the building of its macrostructure.

We should note, however, that the question of building this hierarchy of propositions is still the source of debate. The model we have just described was developed to account for the understanding of narrative texts and bases the construction of the hierarchy of propositions on the recovery of arguments between them. On the other hand, the causal model[5], developed to take account of procedural texts, bases the construction on the causal relationships linking the arguments in the text.

Recent researches[6] have produced experimental results validating both the referential model and the causal model according to the type of text under consideration.

6.1.3 The Mental Model Approach

The mental model approach corresponds to the recent development of the model of van Dijk and Kintsch[7]. It is not strictly structural. It combines the structural approach with a functional approach: in effect, the model envisages a role both for content-rich knowledge schemas as well as for structural schemas. The concept of mental (or situational) model was introduced to account for the role of real world knowledge, knowledge that can take many different forms, generic (knowledge schemas) or episodic. Three levels of representation, distinct but interacting, are identified:

- Level 1: surface representation, also called graphemic or phonemic[8] or 'verbatim representation'[9],
- Level 2: propositional representation (also called 'textbase'),
- level 3: the mental or situational model.

Levels 1 and 2 correspond to linguistic representations of the text and are isomorphic to the structure of the text. They reflect what is contained in the text at a surface and propositional level. Level 3 corresponds to a non-linguistic representation of the text, which reflects the real world situation referred to by the text. This representation is initially constructed from the linguistic representation of the text and makes intensive use of the reader's knowledge of the domain of which the text speaks. This representation is produced by inferences and is itself the source of other inferences. The mental model differs from the level 1 and level 2 models in that it does not reflect the structure of the text. Rather, it is isomorphic to the structure of the situation to which the text refers (as the reader represents it for himself). According to this approach, then, to understand is to construct a detailed representation of the situation.

The propositional representation is constructed by automatic processes starting from the surface representation. Inferences are made but they are automatic and local.

The construction of the mental model is optional. It depends in large part on the conditions under which the reading takes place and its purpose. Building the model is based on the invocation of domain knowledge, as much on semantic and generic knowledge, such as knowledge schemas, as on episodic knowledge, contextualized and specific to a situation encountered in the past. Further, the construction of the mental model takes time and is constrained by the limited capacity of the working memory.

While the story grammar approach and the first propositional models were developed to account for the understanding of narrative texts, these recent developments[10] of Kintsch's model allow the understanding of problem statements and pedagogic texts to be taken into account.

6.2 Program Comprehension Seen as Text Understanding

Researchers who have studied the understanding of software have generally considered a program as a text. This working hypothesis has been largely responsible for the borrowing of theoretical frameworks developed for text understanding, and especially for the three theoretical approaches presented above. These three approaches have produced three quite different perspectives on the understanding of software:

- according to the functional approach, understanding a program is equivalent to applying knowledge schemas;
- according to the structural approach, understanding a program is equivalent to constructing a network of relations;
- according to the mental model approach, understanding a program is equivalent to constructing a detailed representation of the situation.

We shall describe these three approaches and discuss the experimental evidence for each of them and their theoretical limitations.

6.2.1 To Understand a Program Is to Apply Knowledge Schemas

Models/Hypotheses

The central hypothesis of the functional approach is that understanding a program means activating and instantiating knowledge schemas. These schemas represent the generic knowledge that software experts possess. The schemas may be programming schemas or problem schemas. A schema contains variables; it is instantiated when specific values are linked to the different variables (see Chapter 3, Section 3.2).

The two important assumptions of the functional approach to text understanding have been carried over into work on the understanding of software: the importance of knowledge schemas and of top-down processes.

We have seen in the chapter on design that, in the knowledge-centred approach, the expert's generic knowledge has been studied extensively (see Section 3.2). In fact, this approach in terms of schemas has been developed to account as much for the design and production of programs as for their understanding. We recall that, according to this approach, the activity of designing software consists, in part, of retrieving schemas held in memory, suitable for handling certain problems, and instantiating them to produce a program. The activity of understanding consists, in part, of activating schemas stored in memory, using indexes extracted form the program's code, and inferring certain information starting from the schemas invoked.

The second assumption concerns the importance of top-down processing in handling the inputs. Such top-down processes create systems of expectations that make the inputs easier to handle. In fact, the models of software understanding that are classified as functional emphasize bottom-up processes as much as top-down ones. When a schema is activated by an instantiable value of a variable in the schema, expectations are created for the values that can be instantiated into the other variables of the schema, which is to say that these values are inferred. Schema activation mechanisms are described as being either data-driven or concept-driven. In the first case, the activation method is bottom-up; certain information extracted from the code activates a schema or certain elementary schemas already activated invoke in their turn super-schemas to which they are linked. In the second case, the activation mechanism is top-down; super-schemas activate sub-schemas. The schemas invoked cause other, less abstract schemas to be activated.

Brooks (1983) attributes an important role to patterns, in the code or the documentation, which are typical indicators of the presence of certain structures, in particular of instances of schemas; he calls them beacons. When these patterns are identified in the course of reading code, they trigger the activation of corresponding schemas. For example, the presence of instructions to exchange the values of two variables is easily recognizable (see 3.2.2) as an elementary programming schema. When such a sequence of instructions occurs in the middle of a double loop, e.g.

```
for i := 1 to n
        for j := 1 to m
                . . .
                temp := A[i];
                A[i] := A[j];
                A[j] := temp;
                . . .
        end
end
```

an expert will immediately invoke a sort schema.

We can compare this notion of beacons with the notion of focus or focal line described in Section 3.2.2. The focus represents that part of the solution that directly realises the goal of the problem and it thus constitutes the most important part of a schema. It is the most readily available part when a schema is invoked. It is also the part that, during the reading of a program, has the best chance of triggering the activation of a schema. The concept of beacons thus corresponds to the focal part of the code of a program; recognizing a beacon triggers the activation of schemas and of top-down processes, and creates expectations of what else will be found in the program.

Experimental Validation

Two types of experimental validation have been applied to this schema-based approach:

- analysis of the inferences drawn by programmers when reading code and trying to understand it;
- analysis of distortions in recall tasks.

Analysis of Inferences

Inferences drawn while reading code have been studied through two types of experiment: a line by line reading task[11] and a task involving filling in missing lines of code[12].

In order to study some of the inferences made in understanding a program and hence some of the mechanism of understanding, Détienne[13] took up an experimental paradigm developed for studying the understanding of narrative texts[14]. It consists of presenting a text to the experimental subjects, sentence by sentence, and posing questions about the text after each phrase has been presented. This allows information to be gathered on the inferences made by the subjects during the reading of a narrative text. A model can thus be built of the hypotheses that the subject makes while reading, hypotheses constructed by schema activation mechanisms[a].

In a similar way, Détienne presented a program, statement by statement, to expert subjects, asking them after each statement had been presented, to state their hypotheses about the program. Apart from the nature of the material, this procedure is thus identical to that used for studying the understanding of narrative texts. The results illustrate the inferential processes, particularly the activation of schemas[b], used by experts when understanding a program. The verbal protocols have been coded in the form of rules of the form 'if A then B'. These rules represent different mechanisms for using knowledge that allows the subjects to make inferences. The knowledge invoked by the subjects was described in the form of schemas, 'SCHEMAn' being made up of variables 'VARn_m'. The rules identified can be characterized as follows:

- bottom-up rules for activating schemas, expressed in the form 'if VAR1_1 then SCHEMA1' (VAR1_1 is a variable forming part of SCHEMA1) or in the form 'if SCHEMA1_1 then SCHEMA1' (SCHEMA1_1 is linked to a variable forming part of SCHEMA1);
- top-down rules for activating schemas, expressed in the form 'if SCHEMA1 and ... then SCHEMA2' (SCHEMA2 represents a sub-category of SCHEMA1) or in

---

[a]Moreover, the experimenter checked that presenting the text sentence by sentence did not affect the inferential activity. He presented the same texts to subjects who had the task of understanding them, and measured the time taken to read each sentence; the pattern of reading times was compatible with the inference model in the preceding experiment.

[b]When the subjects observe information in the program which was not expected on the basis of the schemas activated, the mechanisms used may be those of schema adaptation.

the form 'if SCHEMA1 **then** SCHEMA1_1 **then** SCHEMA1_2 . . . **then** SCHEMA1_n' (the SCHEMA1_i are linked to variables forming part of SCHEMA_1);

- rules for instantiating schemas, expressed in the form 'if VAR1_1 **then** VAR1_2' (VAR1_1 and VAR1_2 are two variables in the same schema);

- mixed rules that describe an activation mechanism and an instantiation mechanism at the same time. In fact, since the instantiation of a schema begins when the schema is invoked, it is often difficult to distinguish the two. These rules are expressed in the form 'if VAR1_1 **then** SCHEMA1 **then** VAR1_2' (VAR1_1 and VAR1_2 are both variables forming part of SCHEMA1.

Two hundred and sixty-nine rules were identified. They were classified into 47 general rules[c]. In its general form, a rule describes the type of a variable belonging to a schema. In its detailed form, it describes a possible value that will allow the variable to be instantiated.

This data shows the mechanisms of understanding, which are similar to the mechanisms for activating and instantiating schemas described in the literature on the understanding of natural language texts. We shall give three examples in the form of instantiated rules. All the examples are of mixed type. The nature of the variables or the schemas is shown in parentheses.

The first two rules illustrate the activation of a counter schema.

rule 1 for the activation of a counter schema

if VAR1_1 (name of variable): i

if VAR1_2 (type of variable): integer

then SCHEMA1 (variable schema): counter schema

then VAR1_3 (context): iteration

rule 2 for the activation of a counter schema

if VAR1_1(initialization of the variable): i := 1

then SCHEMA1 (variable schema): counter schema

then VAR1_2 (update the variable): i := i+1

Thus a counter schema can be activated by extracting indicators from the code, such as the name of a variable (i), its type, or how it is initialized. The rules also make it clear that the activation of the schema creates expectations, for example, a certain context (iteration) or a certain form of updating (incrementing by 1).

The third example illustrates bottom-up activation of an algorithmic schema for sequential search. We recall that such a schema is made up of more elementary schemas. In this case, the activation is propagated from the elementary schemas to the superstructure, which is the algorithmic schema.

---

[c]The details are given in Détienne, 1986.

rule for activating a sequential search schema

if SCHEMA1_1 (variable schema): counter schema: initialization i :=1; name i

if SCHEMA1_2 (loop schema): while A<>B

then SCHEMA1 (algorithmic schema): sequential search schema

then SCHEMA1_1 (variable schema): counter schema; update i := i+1

In this example, the forms of instantiation of a counter schema and a loop schema invoke an algorithmic schema for sequential search. This activation creates expectations about other values that may be used to instantiate the counter schema.

Soloway and Ehrlich (1984) chose a different experimental paradigm for their study of the inferences that programmers draw when reading a program to try to understand it. They gave their subjects programs from which one line had been omitted and asked them to fill in the blank line with the piece of code that, in their opinion, best completes the program. Their hypothesis was that, if one provided programmers with programs whose structure in terms of plans (instantiations of programming schemas) had been interfered with, this ought to affect the understanding process, especially the invocation of programming schemas by experts.

If this hypothesis is right, then experts would have more difficulty in understanding the 'unplan-like' programs (those whose structure had been interfered with) than the plan-like programs. In contrast, novices should not encounter more difficulties in one case than in the other. The greater or lesser ease of understanding is measured by whether or not the line removed can be correctly inferred from what remains.

In order to test this hypothesis, Soloway and Ehrlich constructed two versions of each of four programs: a plan-like version and an unplan-like version. In the unplan-like versions, the way in which the schemas are instantiated and put together is not typical. Certain rules of programming discourse that control the instantiation of schemas are violated. Figure 6.1 gives an example of the plan-like and unplan-like versions of a program for calculating the average of a set of inputs.

The following results were obtained from the experiment:

- the performance of experts was better than that of novices;

- performance was better on plan-like programs than on unplan-like programs;

- the difference in performance on the plan-like and unplan-like programs was greater for the experts than for the novices.

These results provide experimental support to the hypothesis that experts possess and invoke knowledge schemas to understand programs. The types of error made by the programmers in the unplan-like versions also support this hypothesis; the experts tended to infer prototypical elements of schemas, even for the unplan-like versions. Détienne and Soloway (1990) repeated this experiment but also collected and analysed the subjects' simultaneous verbalizations, which made the expectations created by the invocation of programming schemas very apparent.

These programs calculate the average of a series of numbers read from the input stream. The set is terminated by the sentinel value 99999.

```
{Plan-like version}                            {Unplan-like version}
program Grey(input,output);                    program Orange(input,output);
var     Sum, Count, Num: integer;              var     Sum, Count, Num: integer;
        Average: real;                                 Average: real;
begin                                          begin
        Sum := 0;                                      Sum := -99999;
        Count := 0;                                    Count := -1;
        repeat                                         repeat
            readln(Num);                                   readln(Num);
            if Num<> 99999 then                            Sum := Sum + Num;
                begin                                      Count := Count + 1
                    Sum := Sum + Num;                  until Num = 99999;
                    Count := Count + 1                 Average := Sum/Count;
                end                                    writeln(Average);
            until Num = 99999;                 end.
        Average := Sum/Count;
        writeln(Average);
end.
```

These programs calculate the average of a series of numbers read from the input stream. The set is terminated by the sentinel value 99999.

The plan-like version accomplishes the task in the normal way: variables are initialized to 0; a loop is used to read values and accumulate a running total and a count; the loop is terminated when the sentinel value is detected; the average is then calculated and printed.

The unplan-like version was generated from the plan-like version by violating a rule of programming discourse: *do not use one action for two different purposes in a non-obvious manner*. The initialization actions in this version serve two different purposes:

- they give initial values to Sum and Count;
- the initial values are chosen so as to compensate for the fact that the loop is so constructed that the sentinel value is included in the calculation of the average.

The line ommitted in the experiment, which the subjects were asked to complete, was the initialization of the variable Count (Count := 0 or Count := -1).

Fig. 6.1 Plan-like and unplan-like versions of a Pascal program to calculate the average of a set of numbers (after Soloway and Ehrlich, 1984).

The plan-like version accomplishes the task in the normal way: variables are initialized to 0; a loop is used to read values and accumulate a running total and a count; the loop is terminated when the sentinel value is detected; the average is then calculated and printed.

The unplan-like version was generated from the plan-like version by violating a rule of programming discourse: *do not use one action for two different purposes in a non-obvious manner*. The initialization actions in this version serve two different purposes:

● they give initial values to Sum and Count;

● the initial values are chosen so as to compensate for the fact that the loop is so constructed that the sentinel value is included in the calculation of the average.

The line omitted in the experiment, which the subjects were asked to complete, was the initialization of the variable Count (Count := 0 or Count := -1).

The invocation of schemas facilitates understanding by creating expectations. We must realise, however, that these inference mechanisms can have negative effects in that some of the expectations may turn out not to be satisfied in the actual code. One example of this phenomenon, well known in understanding natural language texts is the difficulty of finding misprints. Expectations are so strong that linguistic information actually present in the text is ignored.

A similar phenomenon has been observed in software[15]. During an experiment in which experts had to read programs written by someone else in order to detect and correct errors, it was noted that the programmers sometimes had difficulty in detecting certain errors. When they had strong expectations that a particular item (i.e. instantiation of a schema variable) would occur in the code, programmers did not systematically process the information that would have allowed them to check that the item was really present in the code; as a result they would fail to detect a different and incorrect instantiation of the variable. This phenomenon is certainly stronger still when the program has been written by the reader himself, who then has even stronger expectations.

Distorted Recall

When subjects are asked to carry out tasks involving recall after reading either texts or programs, two types of distortion bear witness to the effect that knowledge schemas have on understanding[16]: distortions of form and distortions of content. Distortions of form are produced by recalling another possible value of a variable in the schema invoked, in particular a prototypical value, instead of the value with which the variable was really instantiated in the code. Distortions of content, thematic insertions for example, are the result of recalling values inferred from schemas that were not present in the code.

In two experiments carried out by Détienne, expert programmers were given the task of reading a Pascal program, detecting and correcting errors, and then recalling the program. Distortions of form were identified through the recall protocols. We shall give two examples.

The first example concerns the name given to a counter variable. Subjects tended to recall I instead of J. This distortion suggests that a counter schema has been invoked but that the lexical form of the schema variable 'variable name' has not been retained in memory. The subject then recalls another possible value for this variable.

The second example illustrates the recall of a prototypical value of a schema variable instead of its real value. In a 'flag' schema, a schema that allows processing to be terminated when a sentinel value is detected, the schema variable 'context' corresponds to the type of the iteration and can take the values **repeat** or **while**. In one of the programs, a sentinel was used to stop a **repeat** loop. In the course of reading the program line by line, the expected context was systematically taken by all the experts to be a **while** loop (**while not** flag **do**). This suggest that the value **while** is more prototypical than the value **repeat** as an instantiation of the variable 'context' in a flag schema. In the recall phase of the experiment, this prototypical value was recalled by one subject.

The following is an example of distortion of content found in the recall phase. It is a thematic insertion of a value inferred from a stock control schema that had been activated during the reading phase. Such a schema can be formalized as follows:

stock control schema

Problem domain: stock control

Data structure: stock_records (file name, file description) . . .

Functions: allocation (creation or insertion), deletion, search

The 'create' function was difficult to identify in the program to be read, because it was included in a method that supplied other functions as well and did not include the function of creation in its name. Nevertheless, one programmer recalled it as corresponding to a sub-program. It is clear that this value had been inferred on the basis of the stock control schema that had been invoked.

Limitations and Prospects

The theory of schemas seems therefore to be a theoretical framework that allows us to take account of certain phenomena observed during the process of understanding software, especially the process of schema activation. From this point of view, inference seems to work in a very similar way in the understanding of natural language texts and of programs expressed in formal language.

The limitations of this approach are that it does not get to the core of the following issues:

- identification of the control structure between the processes;
- analysis of the more constructive processes in understanding;
- analysis of the processes for evaluating the representations constructed during understanding.

The issue of the control structure between processes is an important one. It goes back to analysing under what conditions the activity of understanding is top-down or bottom-up and what mechanisms are used for adapting known schemas. The direction in which information is processed varies according to the presence or absence of known indicators in the code that are able to activate schemas and according to whether or not the algorithms used are familiar to the subjects or, in other words, whether the subjects already possess schemas with which to understand the program. For example, Widowski and Eyferth (1986) have analysed reading strategies used for what the authors refer to as 'stereotypical' programs. While the understanding process for stereotypical programs is conceptually controlled, for the non-stereotypical programs it is controlled by the data. We shall examine this question in more detail in Section 7.3.

Another issue, intimately linked to the first, is to account for the more constructive processes in the activity of understanding. These mechanisms can typically be studied in situations where the subject is not familiar with the program to be read, possibly through lack of a schema or because the program is unplan-like. In such a case, the subjects certainly have to construct a representation of the relationships between different parts of the code and especially links between elementary plans. For unplan-like programs, inferences based on problem domain principles or on rules of discourse are used, as are mental simulations of the program, using specific data values. The strategy of simulated execution, usually regarded as being followed by beginners, in order to write a program or to work out the goals of a program being read, is used by experts as a way of constructing a representation of an unplan-like program.

Finally, the issue of the processes used to evaluate representations constructed during the understanding activity has been little addressed in the literature. Two evaluation processes can be distinguished:

- checking intra-schema consistency;
- checking inter-schema consistency.

The process of checking intra-schema consistency consists of verifying whether the instantiated values in an instantiation of the schema satisfy any constraints that may apply to the instantiations of variable in that schema. There are two possible types of constraints:

- 'intraslot' constraints, that is, constraints that define the possible values that a variable can take;
- 'interslot' constraints, that is, constraints that link the values taken by different variables: if a variable is instantiated with a value X, it may be that another variable is thereby restricted to being instantiated with a subset of its possible values.

More generally, the rules of discourse may impose inter-variable constraints at a higher level. For example, a program variable that is initialized by an assignment may only be updated by an assignment[d].

Checking inter-schema consistency means checking whether there exist interactions between schemas or, more generally, between the goals that they satisfy, and whether these interactions create constraints on the way the schemas can be instantiated.

6.2.2 To Understand a Program Is to Construct a Network of Relations

According to the structural[e] approach, to understand a program is to construct a network of propositions. This approach highlights the importance of structural knowledge in understanding. We shall consider two versions of this approach: the propositional approach and the structural schema approach.

---

[d]This rule of discourse only applies to straightforward software in non-critical situations. In safety critical systems, for example, there is usually a requirement that all variables should be explicitly initialized, in order to guarantee predictable behaviour.

[e]There is some confusion over terminology. Détienne (1990c) refers to this approach as the control flow approach, which she contrasts with the functional approach that she calls the schema-based approach. Pennington (1987a) contrasts the approach based on 'text structure knowledge' with that based on 'plan knowledge'.

The Propositional Approach and the Importance of Control Structure

The propositional approach to the understanding of programs was inspired by structured programming. The text of a program can be described in terms of a small number of control structures ('control flow units'): sequence, iteration, and selection. These fundamental units have been called prime programs because every program[f] decomposed into a hierarchical combination of them, just as every integer can be decomposed into the product of prime numbers. Depending on their position in the hierarchy, the units may represent the macrostructure (higher in the hierarchy) or the microstructure (the leaves on the tree).

While, according to the functional approach, experts use knowledge schemas, e.g. programming schemas, according to this structural approach it is the role of the structural schemas that predominates. Understanding a program consists in identifying structural units of the sequence, selection and iteration types in the surface structure of the program, and in constructing a structured hierarchical representation at several levels using these units. This view allows proponents of structured programming to claim that programs constructed according to these strict structural rules will be easier to understand and modify because they correspond to the way programmers organize their thoughts[17]. Syntactic markers (see Section 7.2.2), such as **begin-end** for sequences or **for, while,** or **repeat** for iterations, enable programmers to recognize these units in the surface structure of the program. Moreover, these structures have been shown to have a certain psychological reality[18].

Still following this approach, and inspired by the work of Kintsch (1974) on text comprehension, Atwood and Ramsey (1978) hypothesize that the program representation constructed by a programmer is a connected and partially ordered hierarchy of propositions.[g] A proposition is a unit of information that contains one or more arguments plus a relational term. They thus described some FORTRAN statements in propositional terms. Figure 6.2 shows some of the rules they used.

These propositions, derived from the program, are put into relation with each other according to a hierarchical structure. For texts, the connections between propositions are determined by the repetition of arguments. One or more propositions form the 'super-ordinate' propositions in the hierarchy called the 'textbase'. Propositions that share an argument with the super-ordinate propositions form the second level. Propositions that share an argument with the second level proposi-

---

[f]This statement is true only in certain restricted circumstances. It only applies to programs written in procedural languages and then only to those that do not involve such features as exception or interrupt handling. This is still not enough to guarantee that the decomposition will yield a hierarchy; in general it will only yield a graph. However, if appropriate design rules are followed, something close to a hierarchy can be guaranteed.

[g]We note in passing that the authors regard this as a simplification. In fact, they believe that an expert's representation will not be the same as that of a novice. In particular, they bring up the idea of programming schemas, which allow experts to construct code 'chunks' corresponding to known functions such as 'calculate the sum of a table'. Experts do not therefore necessarily construct a propositional representation detailing the structure of control. The authors do not, however, develop these ideas and base their research strictly on the propositional approach. They consider only that chunks correspond to the macrostructure, which is seen as a structural view based on the control structure.

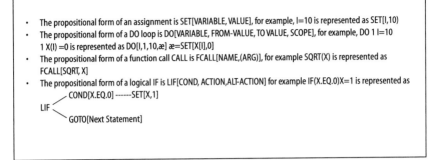

Fig. 6.2 Rules for the propositional analysis of a program.

tions but not with the super-ordinate propositions form the third level. This rule of repetition of arguments is also used for constructing the propositional hierarchy representing a program. One other rule is also applied: propositions that exert control over other propositions are higher in the hierarchy. Thus the higher the level of nesting of a control statement, the lower will be the position of the corresponding proposition in the hierarchy. Figure 6.3 shows an example of a propositional hierarchy, taken from Atwood and Ramsey (op. cit. p. 20). In this representation, the propositions 'CALCULATE TOTAL FREQUENCY' and 'CALCULATE NUMBER OF CATEGORY INTERVALS' represent part of the macrostructure of the program.

The Notion of Role: Towards an Approach In Terms of Structural Schemas

The approach in terms of structural schemas has not been followed explicitly in studying program comprehension. Let us recall that, according to this approach, a text of a certain type (e.g. a scientific article) could be described in terms of a certain structure peculiar to this type of text. A knowledge of these structures, stored in the form of structural schemas could thus direct the process of understanding. Although this approach has not been followed in studying programming, some research on modelling programming knowledge can be approached in terms of story grammars. this is particularly the case with the work of Rist (1986), who introduced the notion of role.

According to Rist, the basic structure of a program is made up of the following roles: input (I), calculate (C) and output (O). Thus a role structure can be related to a structural schema that constitutes the skeleton of a program and also of programming schemas (see Section 3.2.2); for example, a counter schema has the following structure: input role (Count := 0), update role (Count := Count + 1).

These structural schemas certainly depend on the programmers' style, the structuring method followed, and the programming language. Thus, starting from the same programming schemas, a program may be structured by role (e.g. III, CCC, OOO) or by goal (ICO, ICO, ICO).

More generally, Boehm-Davis *et al.* (1992) distinguish different ways in which programs can be structured, such as in-line, functional decomposition, structure by objects. We may suppose that knowledge about these structuring methods is

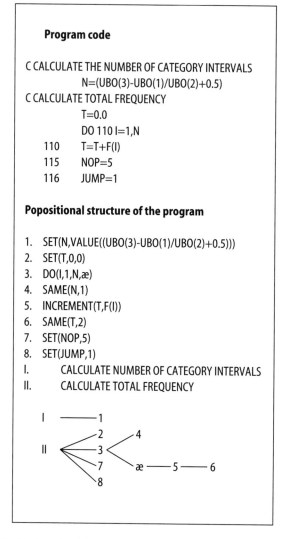

Fig. 6.3 Example of the propositional representation of a programme.

held in the form of structural schemas. One could probably describe structural knowledge relating to programming and, at a more detailed level, to programming languages in this way. For object-oriented programs, in Smalltalk for example, object structural schemas associate a certain number of roles with a generic object: creation, initialization, read access, write access, input, output.

Experimental Validation

The accessibility of the propositions as a function of their position in the propositional hierarchy has been tested in order to provide some experimental support for the propositional approach in programming. Another experimental verification of this approach has been to test a regression model to account for the time taken to read the propositions in the microstructure.

So far as the structural schema approach is concerned, all we can say is that certain results that use a segmentation paradigm are capable of being interpreted in its terms.

Accessibility of Propositions According to Their Position in the Positional Hierarchy

In textual processing, studies[19] have shown experimentally that the probability of recall is inversely proportional to the level of the proposition in the propositional hierarchy: the higher the proposition is in the hierarchy, the greater the probability that it will be recalled. It thus seems that the accessibility of propositions is different, depending on their position in the hierarchy.

Atwood and Ramsey (1978) adapted this experimental paradigm to debugging. They hypothesized that the lower the position of the error in the propositional hierarchy, the more difficult it will be to find it. As a result, more time will be required to find the error. They constructed an experiment in which they varied the position of errors of three types (assignment error, iteration error and error in a table) in the propositional hierarchy. Thus an error of the same type is placed in a proposition high in the hierarchy in one version of the program and in a proposition low in the hierarchy in another version of the same program.

The depth of the error was found to have an effect in only one of the two programs used in the experiment, which limits the value of the result claimed, namely that errors low in the hierarchy were detected significantly more slowly than similar errors occurring high in the propositional hierarchy. A significant interaction between the type of the error and the depth was also found. But the significance of these results is extremely limited because, in the programs used in the experiment, the level in the hierarchy was confused with sequential position in the program text: errors lower in the hierarchy were always situated further down in the text than the same errors higher in the hierarchy. Indeed, the sequential position of the error seemed as good a predictor of the time needed to find the error as its depth.

Vessey (1989) took up the same experimental paradigm but distinguished between the two factors that had been confused. She set out to test two hypotheses formulated by Atwood and Ramsey as a result of their experiments: that the time required to detect an error would be a function of its sequential position in the program and that the probability of detecting an error would be a function of its position in the propositional hierarchy. The results of the three experiments that she carried out do not confirm either hypothesis.

These studies thus provide little experimental evidence in support of the propositional approach. A simpler experimental paradigm using recall might perhaps have been a more direct way of testing the approach. Debugging is a complex activity that is not based solely on comprehension and that brings into play various strategies, as Vessey remarks in her conclusion.

Predicting the Reading Time Using a Regression Model

Regression models have been used successfully to predict reading times in studies of natural language text comprehension[20] and parsing code microstructure[21]. The idea is to determine whether a regression equation will account for a high proportion of the range of variation in reading times. Robertson *et al.* (1990) followed this approach to test the propositional approach to program comprehension. In fact, since they favoured the problem solving approach, they were more concerned to invalidate the propositional approach, by showing that a regression model based on the assumptions of the propositional approach is a good predictor of reading times for isolated statements (in random order in their study), but not of reading times for statements in the correct order in a program.

The regression model used makes the reading time depend linearly on several factors, as follows:

$$Reading\_time = aN_o + bN_v + cN_s + dN_d$$

where

N_o is the number of operators
N_v is the number of variables
N_s is the number of statements
N_d is the number of delimiters

and *a*, *b*, *c*, *d* are the parameters of the model, to be determined from experimental data. It was found that this model accounts for a significant part of the variation when the statements are in random order but not when they are in order. This suggests that the microstructural analysis plays only a weak role in explaining the reading times observed in program comprehension.

Code Segmentation

The program segmentation paradigm has been used as a way of extracting programmers' knowledge. This method has been able to show that programmers remember hold structural schemas in their memories but there has, unfortunately, been no study that shows the effect of these schemas on program comprehension.

Rist (1986) was the first author to use the code segmentation paradigm in programming studies. The method consists of giving programs to experts and novices and asking them to group together and describe instructions that 'go together'. The results obtained with Pascal programs demonstrate that the programmers group the instructions according to roles (which Rist refers to as global plans): initialization, input, processing and output. The same result has been found to be true for FORTRAN programs[22].

The same paradigm has been used[23] with programs written in Smalltalk. This showed that a large part of the grouping is done on the basis of roles: creation, initialization, read access, write access, input, output. It also demonstrated a correspondence between objects and typical functions. Programmers experienced in Smalltalk thus possessed object structural schemas that associate a certain number of roles with a generic object. These schemas bring together the structural features of an object, that is, the data or attributes and the generic characteristics of the functions that are associated with them, i.e. their roles.

Limitations and Prospects

We have to conclude, then, that there has been very little experimental validation of the propositional approach. The studies are not convincing and the results are ambiguous. One theoretical problem is the question of the construction of the hierarchy of propositions. According to Atwood and Ramsey (1978), it depends on the overlapping of arguments between propositions, as in the referential model, and on the control structure – a proposition that controls another will be higher than it in the hierarchy.

Another possible research direction would be to borrow the causal model[24] developed to explain the comprehension of procedural texts. This approach seems, a priori, a very pertinent way of bringing together program comprehension and procedural text comprehension, since a program can be viewed as a procedure written in a special language. According to the causal model the construction of the propositional hierarchy rests on the causal relationships linking the arguments in the text. In a program, the control structure forms one aspect of these causal relationships, in terms of control flow, but we certainly need to add the flow of data and relationships of the condition/action type. So far as we are aware, this theoretical approach has never been used in studying the psychology of programming but it would be an interesting one to explore.

We have seen that the approach in terms of structural schemas or story grammars seems promising and could certainly be one direction for research aimed at explaining program comprehension. But, generally, we believe that any purely structural approach will prove inadequate. Studies of the knowledge of expert programmers (see Section 3.2.1) have shown that they possess content-rich programming schemas, in addition to the structural schemas. Both these types of knowledge probably play their part in program understanding. We shall see that the 'mental model' approach allows these two aspects to be integrated.

6.2.3 To Understand a Program Is to Construct a Representation of the Situation

Models/Hypotheses

According to the mental model approach, to understand a program means to construct a detailed model of the situation. The central hypothesis concerns the distinction between two types of representation that can be constructed when seeking to understand a program: the program model, similar to the concept of the propositional model or the text base used in text comprehension, and the situational model. This distinction harks back to Kintsch's model of text comprehension. This approach has been used to explain the comprehension of procedural programs[25] and, more recently, object-oriented programs[26].

Pennington's Model: the Comprehension of Short Procedural Programs

The program model (or text base) reflects what the program (or text) contains at a propositional level. Two types of relationship are represented at this level: elementary operations and control flow. This representation reflects the information explicit in the text and its structure is isomorphic to the structure of the text.

The domain model (or mental model) reflects the entities of the problem domain and their relationships, that is to say, the problem goals and the flow of data.

The orientation of this approach is strictly bottom-up. It is hypothesized that the program model is constructed first, before the domain model, which emerges later in the comprehension process. Thus the approach maintains a very structural orientation deriving from the propositional approach. It is supposed that the initial representation constructed is of the propositional type. Its construction depends on structural knowledge, especially syntactic and semantic knowledge of the programming language, which allows the flow of control to be analysed into sequences, iterations and selections.

Comprehension of Object-Oriented Programs

In trying to apply Pennington's approach to the comprehension of programs of a different kind, it is found necessary to introduce new concepts and to revise the approach in significant ways. The approach has been extended and revised in order to explain (1) the comprehension of object-oriented programs and not only procedural ones, and (2) the comprehension of long programs and not just short ones.

Pennington's approach takes no account of the representations reflecting the objects or data structures. Objects are, however, entities central to object-oriented programming and the building of the representation of the objects must be taken into account in any model of the comprehension of this type of program[h]. We have hypothesized that the representation of the objects forms part of the situational, in that it reflects the objects of the problem situation.

Pennington's approach explains the comprehension of short programs but cannot easily be applied when the programs are of a more realistic length. In particular, it does not account for two important aspects of long programs: the representation of 'delocalized plans' and the representation of the 'textual macrostructure'.

The approach supposes that programmers use programming schemas to construct situational models. A plan, the instantiation of a schema, is a set of actions that, once they are organized into the correct order, achieve a goal. It also supposes that this representation as a plan is typically based on relationships of the data flow type. In long programs, the plans are often 'delocalized', that is, the lines of code that implement the plan are not positioned contiguously in the program text but are distributed across a number of routines or methods. Furthermore, in OO plans and objects are orthogonal: a plan may make use of several objects and an object may be used in several plans. In an OO system, the actions of a plan are encapsulated in a set of routines; the routines are associated with different classes and are linked through the flow of control. In the approach of Burkhardt *et al.*, the construction of the representation of these complex delocalized plans is considered to be based on the client-server relationship. This relationship accounts for the exchange of data among objects: thus object A is a client of object B when it processes data from object B; object A is a server of B when it provides data to object

---

[h]Indeed, we believe, more generally, that the data structures should be taken into account in the comprehension of any program, be it object oriented or procedural.

B. The representation of this relationship belongs to the situational model inasmuch as its construction depends on the activation of schematic computing knowledge (complex programming schemas).

Pennington's approach does not take into account the macrostructure of large programs at the level of the program model. It accounts for the flow of control between elementary operations but not of the larger textual units such as routines. The approach of Burkhardt *et al.* regards these textual units as constituting the basis of the macrostructure of the program model.

The two approaches thus have in common the fact that they consider the situational model as containing information on the goals and the flow of data. In order to take into account the size and the object-oriented nature of many programs, Burkhardt *et al.* have added information regarding the objects and the client-server relationships. The relationships on the objects and goals represent the static aspects of the situational model, while the data flow and client-server relationships represent its dynamic aspects.

To sum up, then, the program model includes two levels: a micro-level, which represents the microstructure of the program text, and a macro-level, which represents its macrostructure:

- at the level of the microstructure, the elementary operations constitute the basic textual units and the flow of control operations constitute the links between these textual units. The flow of control, at this fine level of granularity, represents the control structure (sequence, loop or test), which link the individual operations;
- at the level of the macrostructure, larger textual units are represented. These are the elementary functions in the program structure, that is to say the routines or methods attached to objects.

The situational model includes both static and dynamic aspects. The static elements of the model are the following:

- the problem domain objects;
- the relations between the objects, that is, the relations of inheritance and composition of objects[i];
- the software objects (or reifed objects) in the Burkhardt *et al.* experiment that do not reflect any object in the problem domain, for example, a string class. These objects are represented at this level because they are necessary to complete the representation of the relations between the problem objects;
- the main goals of the program. they correspond to the functions of the program at a high level of granularity. Most of the time, these high-level functions do not correspond to single units that can be isolated in the program structure. In object-oriented programs, a complex plan that achieves one of the main goals of the program is usually delocalized. The actions of a complex plan are encapsulated in routines attached to different classes and linked among themselves by client-server relationships.

---

[i]Strictly speaking, of course, these relations subsist between the classes to which the objects belong rather than between objects.

The dynamic aspects of the situational model represent communication between the objects at a coarse level of granularity and relations between the variables at a fine level. These relations account for the delocalized plans and the local plans in the program:

- the communication between objects corresponds to the client-server relationship according to which an object processes or supplies data needed by another object. These links connect the different units of a complex delocalized plan. In an object-oriented system, the actions of a complex plan (which implements one of the main goals of the program) are encapsulated in a set of routines, which are distributed across a set of classes and connected by the flow of control. The client-server relationships represent these connections;

- the communication among variables corresponds to data flow relationships. These relations connect the units of the local plans, which are implemented in the routines.

In a manner analogous to text comprehension in natural languages, the construction of the situational model is based on inferences and is also itself the source of new inferences. These inferences are based on the program model and on knowledge of two sorts, generic and episodic, and from two domains, the problem domain and the computing domain. For example, inferences can be made on the basis of programming schemas. Knowledge of the problem situation, whether generic knowledge about a category of problems (problem schemas) or highly contextualized knowledge (episodic knowledge) of a particular problem encountered in the past, can also be activated and be the source of inferences. The construction of the program model, on the other hand, is based on structural knowledge, both syntactic and semantic, and on local inferences for linking propositions among themselves.

One further difference is that Burkhardt *et al.* do not adopt a strictly bottom-up approach. According to them, the construction of the program model does not precede the construction of the situational model: rather, the two models are constructed in parallel and interact with one another. They maintain the important idea that the construction of the program model is systematic and automatic, while the construction of the situational model is optional. This construction requires time and depends on the subject's knowledge and on the reading objective.

Experimental Evidence

The Comprehension/Recall Paradigm

An experimental paradigm of the comprehension/recall type has been used to study the representations constructed during the process of understanding a program[27]. Programmers were asked to read a program for certain period of time (with or without a specific reading objective). Then the program text is taken away from the subject who has then to respond, from memory, to a certain number of questions of the yes/no type[j]. Both the response times and the correctness of the responses are analysed.

The questions posed reflect two different kinds of information:

- information reflecting the program model – elementary operations, flow of control, elementary functions;
- information reflecting the situational model – problem objects, software objects, relations between objects (inheritance or composition), high-level functions (or goals), data flows and client-server relations.

An explicit distinction is made, in line with that used in studies of text comprehension, between three different types of question, according to the type of answer expected: verbatim statements, paraphrases, and inferences. The distinction serves to distinguish:

- questions to which the subject responds on the basis of the propositional model. These are questions demanding verbatim statements or paraphrases as a response;
- questions to which the subject responds on the basis of the situational model. These are questions demanding that valid inferences be drawn from the text read, as well as trick questions about inferences that are plausible but not valid.

We shall see, in fact, that there is an almost total overlap between the type of the relation and the distinction according to the type of answer – verbatim, paraphrase or inference:

- questions about the elementary operations demand verbatim responses. They keep the surface structure of the program;
- the answers to questions about flow of control and elementary functions are paraphrases of information that is explicit in the text;
- questions about objects, relationships between objects, high-level functions (or goals), data flows and client-server relationships, in general require the subject to make inferences[k]. This information is not explicit in the text of the program. It has to be inferred on the basis of information in the text and the programmers' knowledge.

Experimental Validation of Pennington's Approach

Pennington carried out several experiments to test her model. She gave her subjects a relatively short program to read in a limited time and then asked questions reflecting different categories of information considered, in turn, to reflect the program model or the situational model, along the lines indicated above. In a first experiment involving 80 professional programmers, a number rarely reached in studies of this type, she found that after reading a program, whether written

---

[j]The questions are, of course, balanced so that half of the correct responses are affirmative and half are negative.

[k]Note, however, that this is not true of all questions about objects and the relationships between them. Some of the relevant information is explicit in the text. Objects are explicit in an object-oriented program and , what is more, they correspond to the structure of the text. They can also, however, be inferred from the problem schemas. In fact, we believe that this information belongs both to the program model and the situational model. It is also the case that, while certain relationships between objects are explicit, others, for example, certain composition and indirect inheritance relationships, must be inferred.

in Cobol or Fortran, respond better (i.e. with fewer errors) and faster to questions about control flow and elementary operations than to questions about data flow and functions. This analysis thus tends to show that the representations of the flow of control and the elementary operations, which constitute the program model, are constructed first during the process of understanding the program. The representations of the functions and the flow of data, which constitute the situational model, emerge later. Although the analysis of the results of the experiment provides some experimental support for the approach, its generality is in question because the programs used in the study were so short (15 lines).

In a second experiment, Pennington used a longer program (200 lines), with 40 subjects, 20 COBOL programmers and 20 FORTRAN programmers. The experimental procedure comprised two phases: a first phase of reading the program and answering questions, followed by a second phase in which the subjects were asked to modify the program and were then again asked questions. At the end of the first phase, the response patterns were the same as in the first experiment: fewer errors in questions about control flow and elementary operations than in questions about functions and data flows. By contrast, after carrying out the modification task, a different response pattern was observed. Performance in the questions about data flow and functions improved and even exceeded that in questions about the flow of control. One interpretation is that the effect of either the extra time or the modification task has been to change the dominant representation that is constructed to the situational model. Within the framework of her approach, this is interpreted as showing that the construction of the program model precedes that of the situational model.

Pennington also supposes that certain factors, such as the task, can facilitate earlier construction of the situational model. We shall see that Burkhardt *et al.* have shown that this is indeed the case for the OO paradigm.

Experimental Validation of the Approach of Burkhardt et al.

Experimental results have been reported[28] that confirm the cognitive validity of the distinction between program model and situational model in understanding object-oriented programs. The effect of programmer expertise on the construction of these two types of representation has been analysed along with the way the representations evolve over the course of time.

The experimental approach was similar to that used by Pennington in her second experiment, apart from two additional factors, programming expertise[l] and the task (Section 7.1.2). There were two phases: the first phase consisted of reading oriented towards a specific task, either documentation or reuse, followed by questions; the second phase consisted of carrying out the task followed by further questions. The program was some 550 lines long, written in C++. It consisted of ten classes.

First, the experiment showed that, globally, the situational model was more developed (on the basis of correct responses) than the program model. This result, contradicting Pennington's findings for procedural programs, can be interpreted as an effect of the OO paradigm, which facilitates the construction of a situational model.

Another result refers to the effect of expertise. It was hypothesized that the level

---

[l]Thirty experts and 20 beginners took part in the experiment.

of expertise should affect the construction of the situational model but not that of the program model. In fact, the beginners were advanced students who mastered the necessary syntactic and semantic information relatively well and certainly better than the schematic knowledge such as the programming schemas necessary for the construction of the situational model.

On this last point, however, we should note that defenders of the OO approach[29] and its 'naturalness' would make the opposite hypothesis. If problem domain knowledge plays an important role in OO, particularly in the construction of the situational model, one might expect that both programming experts and beginners, when they are equally familiar with the problem domain as was the case in this study, would construct an equivalent situational model. The experimental results however show the opposite and confirm the hypothesis of the experimenters: the situational model constructed by experts is superior to that constructed by beginners but the level of expertise has no effect on the construction of the program model. This suggests that the construction of the situational model depends not only on problem domain knowledge but also on knowledge acquired in the programming domain. This is consistent with the results about OO design[30], which show that experts derive greater benefit from this paradigm than do beginners.

Another research question concerns the order of construction of the two different types of representation, in particular, whether the phase has a different effect on the situational model and the program model. In fact, the situational model is enriched between phase 1 and phase 2 as is attested by the increase in the number of correct responses, while the program model remains stationary. This 'ceiling' effect may be due to the large size of the program, which would make it difficult to hold all the information at this level in the working memory, which has a limited capacity. Another interpretation could be the use of an 'as-needed' reading strategy, which focuses the attention on aspects of the program that are relevant to the task. This point is developed in Chapter 7.

This study shows that there is a certain asymmetry between the static and dynamic parts of the situational model. Globally, the number of correct responses is greater for questions relating to the static than for those relating to the dynamic part. The expertise factor only affects the static part: the static part of the experts' situational model is better developed than that of the beginners. The phase has an effect on both the static and dynamic aspects of the situational model: these two aspects improve over the course of time. Nevertheless, the static part, representing the objects and goals (high-level functions), is always more developed than the dynamic part, which reflects the mental representation of the plans, whether local or complex and delocalized. It seems therefore that the OO paradigm favours the construction of the situational model so far as its static aspects are concerned.

One might expect that the construction of the dynamic part would be important for relating the static aspects of the situational model and the program model. Thus the client-server relationships allow the tracing of a complex plan that performs a high-level function (on the situational model side) and which is made up of elementary functions (on the program model side); they thus set up a relationship between structures that are not isomorphic. The results of this study thus suggest that the OO paradigm does not facilitate the setting up of relationships between these two representations, at least not in the initial phases of comprehension.

Limitations and Prospects

The theoretical approach that distinguishes the program model and the situational model seems to be applicable quite well to program comprehension and has received convincing experimental confirmation. Further research is, however, necessary to deepen the insights that can be gained from this approach.

One theoretical question is whether the model of Burkhardt *et al.* can be applied more generally to all types of program by distinguishing between the more generic mechanisms and those that are linked to the features of specific programming languages.

From a theoretical point of view, this approach is interesting because it accounts for the use of various types of knowledge: structural knowledge (in the sense of control structure) and knowledge schemas in both the problem domain and the software domain. Another interesting theoretical point is that it explains the effect of the reading objective on comprehension. A program is always read with a specific reading objective such as modification. We shall see in the next chapter that this theoretical approach allows us to interpret the effect of the task on the representations constructed in program comprehension.

6.3 Program Comprehension Seen as Problem Solving

As stated by some authors[31], the problem solving paradigm would be a better theoretical framework for explaining program comprehension than the text comprehension framework. According to such an approach, program comprehension would square with mechanisms for problem solving and plan recognition. The authors underline the importance of the selection processes and the selective character of the representations constructed in program comprehension.

The work of Gilmore and Green (1984a, 1984b) on program comprehension can also be viewed as falling into the problems solving framework. They consider that the cognitive processes put to work in order to understand a program are determined by the task to be carried out. These mental operations involve searching for information relevant to carrying out the task. The authors are explicitly opposed to the propositional approach according to which, whatever the task at which the comprehension is aimed, the representation constructed will be the same.

Two experimental paradigms have been used to validate this approach experimentally: the analysis of strategies and reading times, and the performance of various tasks.

One argument in favour of the problem solving approach is that programmers read the code in a non-linear way; these reflects some decision taking and, more generally, reasoning processes used when reading. Robertson *et al.* analysed the reading strategies of experienced programmers. A program written in Pascal was presented, statement by statement, on the screen. By pressing special keys subjects could view previous and subsequent lines and, also , could jump to the beginning of the previous or the next procedure. The order in which the statements were read and the time taken to read each statement were recorded.

This study shows that, when a program is relatively long (136 statements in this case), it is not read linearly. In this experiment, 11 per cent of the reading activity consists of changing the direction of reading; of this, most involved jumping ahead. The changes of direction are characterized by longer reading times, which, according to the authors, reflect the decision taking mechanisms. The longest reading times are associated with the changes of direction that involve going backwards; this reflects the taking of decisions concerning the re-examination of Sections of code or the search for specific information.

In another experiment, in which the subjects had to modify a program, it was found that scarcely half the code was really read, which clearly demonstrates the selective character of the reading process. Information relevant to the task in hand is sought out and reading is focused on such information.

According to Gilmore and Green, the mental operations used in understanding a program depend on the task to be carried out. They are information selection processes that depend on the relevance of the information to a given task. Certain programming languages emphasize certain types of information while other languages emphasize other types. Thus, for example, declarative languages emphasize circumstantial information while procedural languages emphasize sequential information. The authors hypothesize that the information selection procedures are easier when the language and the task to be carried out[m] are compatible. According to the propositional model, in contrast, it is expected that, whatever the language, the same type of mental representation is constructed; in this case, the language would have no effect on the processes of information extraction.

Gilmore and Green made a comparative study of a declarative language and a procedural language. They hypothesized that the notational structure of procedural languages emphasizes sequential information, i.e. what action is performed after action X, while the notational structure of declarative languages emphasizes circumstantial information, i.e. under what conditions is action X performed. Subjects should thus respond more easily to sequential questions when they refer to a program written in a procedural language while they should respond more easily to circumstantial questions when they refer to a program written in a declarative language. This hypothesis is confirmed by the experimental results: performance is better when the notational structure of the language is compatible with the demands of the task. This result emphasizes the importance of the information selection process in program comprehension aimed at a specific task.

When the language and the task are not compatible, Gilmore and Green hypothesize that the addition of notational markers relevant to the task to be carried out can improve performance. They set up experiments in which sequence markers were added to the programs in the declarative language and condition markers to the programs in the procedural language. Performance ought to be improved when these markers are relevant to the task and there is incompatibility between the task and the notational structure. This hypothesis was partly confirmed by the experimental results.

---

[m]Note that this is the task in the sense in which it has been used earlier, i.e. modification, documentation, reuse, etc., *not* the task in the sense of the goal of the program.

The studies we have described provide some experimental confirmation for this theoretical approach. It is important, however, to underline the theoretical limits of this approach. The authors all contrast the problem solving approach with two approaches in terms of text comprehension: the purely functional approach and the purely structural approach. They do not discuss the mental model approach. It seems to us, however, that this last approach accounts equally well for the phenomena on which the authors base their theoretical orientation. Indeed, the mental model approach explains the problem solving mechanisms: they are inferences made in order to construct the situational model and processes of selective encoding. Further, the authors who defend the problem solving approach have a somewhat simplistic view of current models of comprehension. They suppose, wrongly, that these models do not explain variations in strategy, linked to the task. We shall see in the next chapter that the mental model approach is, on the contrary, a theoretical approach that potentially has the predictive and explanatory power to account for how the comprehension activity is determined by the task (or reading objective).

6.4 Conclusions and Practical Implications

Each theoretical approach has been the subject of several experimental validations and accounts for certain phenomena observed in program comprehension. In conclusion, it seems necessary to recognize a certain complementarity among the different theoretical approaches to program comprehension. Each approach is centred on certain processes:

- the functional approach emphasizes the mechanisms for invoking knowledge schemas, programming schemas and the problem schema;
- the structural approach emphasizes the importance of structural schemas;
- the mental model approach the two previous aspects by distinguishing two representations constructed during the process of comprehension: the program model, a proposition model and the situational model, constructed by inferences, based especially on programming schemas and the problem schema. This approach allows the effect of the reading objective to be explained;
- the problem solving approach emphasizes the importance of the information selection mechanisms in program comprehension aimed at a specific task or reading objective.

It appears that the mental model approach is the one that explains most completely the processes employed and the representations constructed in the course of understanding a program. We shall see in the next chapter that this approach is equally interesting for explaining the effect that the task to be carried out has on the process of comprehension.

These different approaches have many practical implications. According to the functional approach, it is important to facilitate the recall of programming schemas in order to make comprehension easier. Several paths seem promising, some of which will be developed in the next chapter:

- construct canonical programs that comply with the rules of programming discourse;
- emphasize focal lines or beacons;
- in the documentation or the titles of routines, provide information that will help to invoke the appropriate schemas.

According to the structural approach, it is important to facilitate the invocation of structural schemas in order to make comprehension easier. We have seen that the approach in terms of structural schemas or story grammars seems promising and could also be a research line for explaining comprehension. From the point of view of applications like program editors, this approach could certainly provide very valuable information for generating or recognizing program structures.

We have seen that, according to the mental model approach, a programming model and a situational model are both constructed during the comprehension process; it is only the construction of the situational model that distinguishes experts from novices. It is certainly possible to facilitate its construction by providing suitable documentation (see Chapter 7).

References

1. Galambos, Abelson and Black, 1986; Schank and Abelson, 1977.
2. Meyer, 1975; Mandler and Johnson, 1977.
3. Norman and Rumelhart, 1975; Kintsch, 1974.
4. Van Dijk and Kintsch, 1983.
5. Trabasso and Suh, 1993.
6. Bergfeld-Mills, Diehl, Birkmire and Mou, 1993, 1995.
7. Kintsch, 1988.
8. Johnson-Laird, 1983.
9. Schmalhofer and Glavanov, 1986.
10. Kintsch, 1988, 1992, 1994.
11. Détienne, 1986.
12. Soloway and Ehrlich, 1984.
13. Détienne 1986a; 1988.
14. Rumelhart, 1981.
15. Détienne, 1984.
16. Détienne, 1990b.
17. Dahl, Dijkstra and Hoare, 1972, quoted in Pennington, 1987a.
18. Adelson, 1981; McKeithen, Reitman, Reuter and Hirtle, 1981.
19. Kintsch and Keenan, 1973.
20. Haberlandt and Graesser, 1985.
21. Mayer, 1987.
22. Roberston and Yu, 1990.
23. Chatel and Détienne, 1994; Chatel, 1997.
24. Trabasso and Suh, 1993.
25. Pennington, 1987a, 1987b.
26. Burkhardt, Détienne and Wiedenbeck, 1997.
27. Burkhardt, 1997; Burkhardt, Détienne and Wiedenbeck, 1997; Pennington 1987a, 1987b.
28. Burkhardt, 1997, 1998.
29. Borgida, Greenspan and Mylopoulos, 1986; Meyer, 1988; Rosson and Alpert, 1990.
30. Détienne, 1997.
31. Koenemann and Robertson, 1991; Robertson, Davis, Okabe and Fitz-Randolf, 1990.

7. *Understanding Software: Effects of the Task and the Textual Structure*

■ ■

Program comprehension is characterized by the fact that, in seeking to understand a program, the reader always has a task in mind or, according to the terminology used in textual comprehension, a purpose for reading (or reading objective). We shall define a typology of purposes for reading, depending on whether the goal is to recall or to act on a situation. This typology has been developed for textual comprehension within the framework of the model of van Dijk and Kintsch and we shall discuss its relevance to program comprehension.

The textual structure also has an important effect on the process of understanding, both in itself and through its interaction with the task at which the understanding is directed. We shall develop this point in Section 7.2.

■ ■

7.1 Influence of the Task

A programmer usually seeks to understand a program in order to carry out a specific task such as modification, reuse, debugging or documentation. It is therefore necessary that any model of program understanding takes the influence of that task into account.

In text comprehension, this question leads to the study of the effect of the purpose for reading. Only the 'mental model' approach, notably the recent extension of the model by Kintsch and van Dijk, takes into account the effect of the purpose for reading. We shall explain how this model works. We shall then borrow a typology of purposes for reading from studies of text comprehension, in particular the distinction between 'read-to-recall' and 'read-to-do'. We shall use this typology to describe studies of program comprehension aimed at a specific task. This will allow us to suggest some theoretical enrichment to this approach to text comprehension.

7.1.1 Effect of the Purpose for Reading on Text Comprehension

The purposes for reading used in experimental studies of text comprehension have classically been: summarize, recall, and answer questions. These objectives are not very realistic and lead more to the memorisation of text than to its comprehension in the strict sense. In more recent studies, mostly based on Kintsch's model, purposes for reading concerned with acting on a situation have been used: execute (in the case of instructions), solve a problem, or learn to handle a new situation. In particular, these studies have allowed us, on the one hand, to distinguish what is involved in memorising text from what is involved in understanding it, and, on the other hand, to enrich the concept of mental model or situational model.

In its recent form, the mental model approach takes into account the effect of the purpose for reading on text comprehension. Two major categories of purposes for reading are distinguished[1]: 'read-to-recall' and 'read-to-do'. Experimental studies have shown that these two types of purpose for reading have different effects on the encoding processes used in text comprehension and on the type of representation constructed.

One hypothesis is that read-to-recall will focus the activity of comprehension on constructing the propositional model (that is, on what is said in the text and how it is said) while read-to-do will focus on constructing the mental or situational model (that is, on the situation referred to). In a study[1] in which they compared two groups of subjects to whom they had given one or other of these objectives, Bergfeld-Mills *et al.* (1995) showed that subjects with the first objective recalled a procedural text better while subjects with the second objective recalled the procedure described in the text better. The read-to-do group recalled the information considered less important for carrying out the procedure less well than the read-to-recall group. These results thus provide empirical validation of the hypothesis of the differential effect of the purposes for reading.

In another study[2], the read-to-recall objective was operationalised by the instruction to make a summary of the text and read-to-do was operationalised by the instruction to acquire knowledge. The subjects had to read a programming manual with one of these objectives. It was found that the subjects who were reading in order to produce a summary recalled more propositional information while those who read to learn recalled more situational information.

Another, complementary, hypothesis is that different encoding processes are put to work depending on the purpose for reading. The Bergfeld-Mills study shows that the reading times varied according to how important the information was for carrying out the task described in the text. They varied more for subjects reading to do than for those reading to recall. The Schmalhofer study showed that patterns of reading times differ depending on the purpose for reading. Subjects instructed to read to learn read faster, and with different patterns of reading time, in comparison with subjects instructed to read in order to make a summary. This is to be expected insofar as the subjects who read to make a summary (read-to-recall) most concentrate on all the information in the text, which is not the case for those who are reading to learn (read-to-do). These different results confirm the hypothesis that the encoding process differs according to the purpose for reading.

7.1.2 Effect of the Task on Program Comprehension

A program is always read with a purpose for reading, for example, to modify the program (in a maintenance task) or to reuse it. These natural situations offer the opportunity of studying the effect of these purposes for reading on the processing of procedural texts such as computer programs. According to the mental model approach, the purpose for reading has an effect on the encoding process and on the type of representation constructed, that is, whether it is a propositional model (or program model) or a situation model. Two types of task can be considered as examples of the read-to-recall objective: documentation tasks and memorising tasks in the strict sense. Tasks that correspond to the read-to-do' objective are program modification and reuse.

Read-To-Recall

Two studies by Pennington[3] illustrate the effect that a recall task in the strict sense has on comprehension. In her first study, the programmers were instructed to read a program that they would have to recall later. In the first phase of her second study, they had to read a program in order to modify it later. But the modification task was only specified in the second phase. After the first phase of reading, the subjects had only to reply to questions on the program. In these two studies, the experts answered questions on the flow of control better than questions on the purpose of the program. These results thus provide an empirical validation of the hypothesis that a program model type of representation is constructed. We should note that subjects with a yet unspecified modification task in fact construct the same type of representation[a].

Reading a program written by someone else, in order to document it, can be considered to fall into the read-to-recall category studied in text comprehension. Indeed, it is quite similar to the task of making a summary. One can therefore expect that the documentation objective will cause the reading to focus on the construction of a program model[b].

A working hypothesis in studying[4] the task of documenting a program written by someone else is that the documentation produced reflects the cognitive representation that the programmer constructs of the entity that she or he is documenting. Analysis of the documentation produced allows us to identify several categories of information: paraphrases (some documentation paraphrases the instructions in the program and carries no additional information), syntactic explanations (relating to programming rules), semantic explanations (concerning the solutions adopted), and meta-documentation (comments about the documentation itself). This result indicates that the representation constructed in a documentation task reflects (1) information on the low-level functions, close to those that Pennington calls the elementary operations and we have termed semantic explanations, and (2) information on the flow of control (in the paraphrases). This tends to confirm that the documentation reflects the programmer's program model.

Another interesting result is that the structural units, for example, the opening of loops, are the units most frequently annotated. This suggests that the structure

---

[a]Similarly, it has been shown (Burkhardt, Détienne and Wiedenbeck, 1997; 1998) that the orientation of the task has no effect on the representation constructed but that the carrying out of the task does.
[b]Documenting a program already written, and often written by someone else, is to be distinguished from the situation in which a programmer documents his own program while designing and coding it. In this latter case, the documentation goes from the justification of high level design decision all the way down to the description of implementation details. It is clear in this case that the representation constructed (to the extent that it is reflected in the type of documentation produced) is not limited to the program model (Détienne, Rouet, Burkhardt and Deleuze-Dordon, 1996).

of the representation constructed reflects the structure of the program text as it is defined by the control structure. This again tends to confirm that it is a program model rather than a situation model that the experimental subjects have constructed.

Another study of documentation[5] has shown that, when expert programmers are documenting a program written by someone else, they produce twice as many detailed comments, referring to explicit instructions in the code, as abstract comments, referring to the problem. Furthermore, the vertical spacing of the comments tends to reflect the textual structure of the program, with comments being placed between routines, for example. These results again tend to confirm that it is a program model that is being constructed.

Read-To-Do

There are several different tasks that can be used to examine the effect of a purpose for reading of the read-to-do type, modifying or reusing a program, for example. In these situations, the programmer reads a program in order to use the information extracted or inferred to accomplish a task. When a program is to be modified, the task requires new specifications to be taken into account. The program being read must be modified to satisfy new constraints or new goals. In the case of reuse, the source program is reused to design or implement the solution to a new problem, the target. Two important results have come out of the study of modification and reuse. We shall see that, just as in text comprehension in natural languages, one finds that a read-to-do objective affects the encoding processes and involves the construction of a model of the situation.

Several studies of modification tasks[6] have shown that special encoding processes are used. Programmers make use of 'as-needed' strategies. In other words, they study only those parts of the code or of the documentation that they consider relevant to the task. Three levels of relevance can be distinguished:

- direct relevance, that is, the parts of the code that will have to be changed;
- intermediate relevance, that is, the parts that are seen as interacting with the code that has to be modified;
- strategic relevance, that is, the parts that serve more or less directly to position relevant code.

One objective of read-to-do is to focus the comprehension activity on constructing a model of the situation. This has been empirically verified[7] in the case of program understanding for the purpose of modification. The first phase of the experiment consisted of reading a program which was to be modified later, the modifications required having not yet been specified. The second phase consisted of actually making the modifications. Once they had made the modifications, the programmers responded better to questions about the purpose of the program than to questions about the flow of control. It thus seems that carrying out a modification task entails building a model of the situation. The extent to which this result can be interpreted and generalized is, however, limited because the experimental paradigm used confused the effect of the task and the effect of the additional time available for reading the program.

The effect of reading programs in order to reuse them has been studied in an object-oriented context[8]. Two groups of programmers, with different levels of programming expertise, were compared. It was found that there was an interaction between the type of model constructed, the task and the level of expertise. For the novices, who were advanced students, it is clear that the reuse task entails enriching the model of the situation obtained from the source program. Thus the reuse task turns the building of the model of the situation into the focus of the comprehension activity. The model thus obtained is just as rich as that constructed by experts, whatever the task. For the experts, the situation model constructed before carrying out the reuse task is already fairly rich. In contrast, carrying out the reuse task entails focusing on the functional relationships, especially a representation of the goals and sub-goals, which link the situation model (problem goals) and the program model (sub-goals or functions corresponding to the structural units of the program).

It has further been shown[9] that, when they are reusing a source class, expert programmers make use of the context in which the class is used in an example program. This result can also be interpreted as building a situation model, in particular, constructing the functional relationships between the class being reused and the other classes of the example program.

What these studies demonstrate is, on the one hand, that the effect of reuse on the comprehension process is to focus attention on the construction of a situation model and, on the other hand, that experts also construct a representation that links the situation model to the program model. This second result needs to be seen in the context of object-oriented programming, insofar as the complex plans and the objects are orthogonal and it is therefore difficult to get an idea of the functional relations that link one class to the other classes of the program. Experts construct such a representation, which is essential for reusing classes and the functionality of a source program.

7.1.3 Research Prospects

We have shown how the mental model approach allows the effect of the task to be taken into account in text comprehension and we have extended this approach to program comprehension. This has produced new results concerning the interactions between the type of model constructed, the task, and the level of expertise of the programmer. Studies of text comprehension have considered both the effect of the task and the effect of expertise but they have not studied the combined effect of these two factors. In order to make progress in this problem area, further research is needed to discover how expertise in the reference domain and expertise in the task affect comprehension;

From the point of view of the psychology of programming, however, we need to refine the classification of programming tasks, at present based on the fairly loose classification commonly used in software engineering. We saw in Section 4.3 that the reuse task can be classified on several cognitive dimensions. It would be valuable to make use of this classification to study the comprehension process when reuse is the goal. We saw that reuse mechanisms differ according to whether the reuse occurs in the analysis phase, the problem-solving phase, or the coding phase. It is probable that the purpose for reading will also differ according to the phase in which the reuse occurs. In the analysis and problem-solving phases, the purpose for reading is likely to be of the read-to-do type, with attention concentrated on constructing a model of the source situation, which will have the effect of enriching the representation of the target as we saw in Section 4.3.2. In the coding phase, the purpose for reading will be of the read-to-recall type, focusing attention on the construction of a model of the source program, which will have the effect of lowering the level of control of the activity as we saw in Section 4.3.

7.2 Effect of the Textual Structure

Natural language text has a linear structure while a mental or situational model constructed during the process of comprehension is multi-dimensional. Similarly, a computer program has a linear structure (surface or textual structure) while the situational model (deep structure) is multi-dimensional. One research question is to account for the way in which this surface structure is transformed into deep structure. The process of delinearisation is one of the cognitive processes that allows us to pass from the surface structure to a representation of the deep structure. This process is influenced by the textual structure[10]. We analysed earlier (Chapter 6) the role played by the experimental subjects' knowledge in making inferences that help to construct the situation model. We shall now analyse the role of the textual structure in this process of delinearisation, which is one of the processes used to construct the situation model.

7.2.1 Surface Structure vs Deep Structure

The surface structure corresponds to the textual structure of the program. According to the mental model approach to program understanding (see Section 6.2.3), the surface units correspond to (1) the elementary operations, (2) the functional units such as procedures and functions, and (3) units defined by the control structure. Two types of ordering are explicit in the surface structure: the linear ordering of the elementary operations and the order of execution implied by the control structure.

The deep structure corresponds to the situation model. The static or declarative aspects of the situation model are the objects (or, more generally, the data structures) and the principal goals of the program. The dynamic or procedural aspects of the model are: the call links between methods (client-server links in OO), which connect the elements of complex plans, these plans achieving the principal goals, and the flows of data that link the elements of simple plans.

7.2.2 Organizers

Advance Organizers: Titles and Initial Comments

An advance organizer is a textual element, such as a title or a comment, that is presented before the text that is to be read. This type of organizer has a considerable influence on the interpretation that the reader will construct when reading the text that follows. Titles are considered to be a particular type of advance organizer and to be powerful tools for establishing a theme. One of the principal functions of titles is to indicate the hierarchical structure of the message being conveyed, which is of particular importance in procedural texts. The presence of titles especially facilitates identification of the important ideas in the text, division of the text into chunks – smaller blocks of information, and identification of changes of topic.

In programming, we can compare the role of initial comments to the role of titles. Thus attempts have been made to decide which types of comment are useful and where they should be placed. The comments used describe the function implemented by a Section of code and are placed before the Section. We would therefore expect that comments would have two effects. By virtue of their physical positioning, they will serve to identify groups of statements contributing to the same goal and thus help with the process of 'chunking'. By the meaning that they express, they serve to invoke acquired knowledge or content-rich schemas. Activating existing knowledge in this way, before looking at the code itself, facilitates the processes of building a representation.

Two types of study have been carried out into the effect of titles (that is, meaningful names given to procedures and functions) or initial comments on program comprehension: some studies have used a recall task or the performance of a programming task as an indicator of comprehension; other studies have used the inference processes that take place when the program is being read. We shall see that whether or not the advance organizers have a visible effect depends on the type of the experiment.

Studies that use an experimental method measuring the effect of advance organizers on recall performance[11] or on a debugging task[12] show no evidence of a positive effect on the programmers. The expert, however, even in the absence of titles or meaningful comments, makes use of other information in the code in order to build a representation. Even though one might think that these processes for building a representation are different and longer, the effect is certainly not visible in terms of recall performance or debugging.

In contrast, studies that use an experimental method that takes into account the processes of constructing a representation[13] show that advance organizers have a visible effect. Détienne (1986) analyses the inferences made by programmers in the course of reading a program presented to them line by line, a method that allows the intake of information to be controlled. This analysis shows that the names of procedures and functions allow inferences to be drawn about the purpose of the functional block that follows and allows content-rich knowledge schemas to be activated.

Norcio's study makes very apparent the double effect of the physical layout and the initial comments on the process of chunking and the process of activating knowledge schemas. He studied the effect of functional comments placed between the functional segments. The experimental subjects were given the task of filling in lines missing from the code. Indenting programs on the basis of functional units identified by expert programmers facilitated comprehension. Subjects faced with an indented program completed it significantly more correctly than subjects faced with a program without indentation. Furthermore, when there is an initial comment the performance is better, especially when completing an initial line of code, than without the comment.

Textual Organizers: Linkage Markers, Boundaries

In models of text comprehension, the paragraph is defined as any passage marked in the surface structure by two indented lines, independently of the content. It has a threefold psychological status: an indication of the cognitive structure of the writer, a constituent part of the text, and a processing unit for the reader.

Two types of textual structure can define analogues of the paragraph for the reader of a program: procedures or routines, and the structural units linked to the control structure (iteration, test, sequence). These are the processing units during reading, which are marked in particular by changes of reading direction accompanied by pauses.

The order in which the instructions of a program written in Pascal are read has been analysed[14]. Changes in the direction of reading correspond mainly to:

- linkage markers of control units (first line of a control structure), 23 per cent;
- linkage markers for procedures, 21 per cent.

Of the remaining changes of reading direction, 18 per cent result from following the flow of data (by means of a variable name) and 10 per cent from the functional units internal to procedures. Thus the boundaries of the textual units such as the control units or pseudo-paragraphs play a very special role in reading a program. Other types of link are also followed, notably the data flow that shows the plan.

Thematic Organizers: Beacons

The textual structure gives readers information about the hierarchical structure of the content of the text and influences the way they process the material when reading it. It has been shown[15] that two different presentations of the same information content can lead to different performances on the part of the readers. The delinearizing process is made easier by the presence of signal, for example, a word or phrase in a text that adds no new information to the topic but accentuates certain aspects of the semantic content. They permit the reader who is sufficiently expert to place the items of information contained in the text into a hierarchy and thus to attribute primary or secondary importance to them.

In programming, as we have seen, some of the items of information contained in a programming schema may be more important than others, because the information is essential in achieving the goal of the schema. We have already met this idea, under the name of focus, in Section 3.2.2. Schemas can be described[16] in terms of a structural hierarchy where the foci are at the higher (and therefore more important) levels of the hierarchy. Certain pieces of code in program text, called 'beacons' by Brooks (1986), are instances of foci. We can thus see these beacons as thematic organizers, which will allow knowledge schemas to be activated and important information to be distinguished from secondary information.

It has been shown[17] that experts recall beacons better than other lines of program but that novices do not. This suggests strongly that beacons play an important role in building a hierarchy from the information in the program.

Extra-Textual Organizers

The idea of extra-textual organizers harks back to the structural schemas or textual superstructure, introduced in Section 6.1.2, which allow readers to recognize the conventional organization of different types of text. The knowledge and activation of the superstructure for a given type of text, for example, the principles on which this type of text is organized, facilitate the processing of the macrostructure of the propositional representation of the text. These structural schemas allow the reader to put to work specific strategies adapted to that type of text.

We discussed the idea of role in programming and its interpretation in terms of structural schemas on Section 6.2.2. Several studies[18] have identified constituent elements of such schemas in different programming languages. So far as we are aware, only one study[19] suggests elements that may have a bearing on the way that a knowledge of structural schemas affects the understanding of a program. Different features of the program representations constructed by experts and novices in an understanding and recall task were analysed. While many features are dependent on expertise, experts and novices locate structural information in the text of the program equally easily: for example, finding the variable declarations in a procedure in a Pascal program. This indicates that programmers possess structural schemas, acquired very early in the learning process, which enable them to use the program structure to locate certain information.

7.2.3 Discontinuities and Delocalized Plans

In text comprehension, there are two principles that account for difficulties in understanding a procedural text (especially one consisting of instructions to be carried out): referential discontinuities and the ordering principle.

One of the major determinants of the local coherence of a text is the ease with which multiple references to the same individual or object can be followed. The commonest way of making it easy to follow such references is to ensure referential continuity between successive sentences. Studies show[20] that referential discontinuities cause difficulties in understanding. Adults who have been asked to read and follow instructions for assembling a three dimensional object arrive at a correct configuration more often when the descriptions are continuous than when they include referential discontinuities.

The ordering principle requires that the order in which information is mentioned in the instructions corresponds to the order in which the instructions are executed. The lack of such a correspondence causes difficulties in understanding. Instructions whose structure corresponds to their order of execution (antecedents, actions, consequences) are read more rapidly and recalled better than those that do not respect the ordering principle. This suggests that optimal performance is achieved when the coding of the statements corresponds to the temporal and spatial coding of the situations described. This principle can be interpreted in terms of the theory of schemas: understanding a simple instruction is effected by instantiating variables of a schema. The reading time will thus be shorter if the surface structure of the statements corresponds to the structure of schema.

The difficulties experienced in understanding certain program can be interpreted in terms of these referential discontinuities and violations of the ordering principle. A plan corresponds to the instantiation of a schema in the text of a program. Often, the different lines of code that make up a single, complex plan are scattered through the program, that is to say, they are not in strictly linear order, whether they are intermingled with lines of code corresponding to other plans or whether that are divided among different functional units of the program. Such a plan is described as 'delocalized'; formally it can be defined as a plan whose code is distributed non-contiguously in a program. We should note that the notational structure of the programming language has an influence on the delocalization of plans. Thus OO languages involve a very strong delocalization of plans, which may be distributed through several procedures, each attached to different classes.

It has been observed[21] that programmers engaged in maintaining a procedural program that they haven't written themselves do not understand the interactions between parts of the code remote from one another, all the more so if these interactions are not documented. The tendency was rather to interpret each part of the code in the local context. It has also been shown[22] that, when trying to understand OO programs, experts have difficulties in building a representation of client-server relationships that link parts of a plan distributed across several classes. Finally, recent work[23] suggests that delocalization substantially reduces the effectiveness of program inspection in an object-oriented environment.

7.2.4 Research Prospects

In a recent extension of the mental model approach to textual understanding, Zwaan, Magliano and Graesser (1995) have analysed the multi-dimensional nature of the situational model more deeply. They distinguish three dimensions along which one characterize situational continuity in a text: the temporal dimension, the spatial dimension, and the causal dimension. Discontinuities in the text along any one of these dimensions provoke understanding difficulties, especially difficulties in producing the situation model or deep structure of the text. Temporal discontinuities manifest themselves in the form of jumps in time, forward or backward, between two contiguous sentences in the text, for example, 'an hour later'. Spatial discontinuities occur when the actions described by two contiguous sentences take place in spatially different environments. Causal discontinues arise when the likely cause of an event cannot be identified from the context preceding its description.

It would be useful to investigate the relationship between these different types of discontinuity and the cognitive dimensions used to characterize programming languages, discussed in Section 3.3.2. The idea of temporal discontinuity, for example, has an obvious connection with the type of discontinuity introduced by **goto** statements. Causal discontinuities might be related to exceptions and exception handlers.

7.3 Practical Implications

We have seen that, depending on the nature of the task, the type of representation constructed will be a program model, a situation model, or a model that links the two representations. The construction of these different types of representation will be easier or harder depending on the notational structure of the language and the expertise of the reader. Thus novices have much more difficulty building a situational model than do the experts, while they build a program model just as easily. Thus it is absolutely essential to produce documentation that makes explicit the information that is implicit in the program code. It is necessary to arrange for the documentation to make explicit various types of information relating to the situational model and also the text model, as well as the relationships between the different types of information[24].

The documentation should also be related to the notion of organizers. We have seen that different features of the textual structure have an effect on understanding. Highlighting them, using suitable visualization tools, should lead to a better understanding of different aspects of the program, linked to the content and the deep structure (beacons for programming schemas) as well as to the textual superstructure (role and structural schemas).

Help in understanding delocalized plans might be envisaged in two forms: by the provision of suitable documentation that links, and explains the links, between the physically separated parts of the plan; and by tools that can follow delocalized plans and thus help to visualize the plan in its entirety. So far as the first of these is concerned, it has been suggested[25] that variables should be documented in a way that distinguishes their role and purpose; the role shows the type of data that a variable can be used for while its purpose relates to its function at the level of the plan in which it participates. Modern programming languages with user-defined types provide a mechanism for making clear the role of the variable; it is also common but by no means universal practice to document the variable with a description of its function. So far as tools are concerned, tools might be provided that allow plans to be visualized through data flow relationships and through client-server relationships.

References

1. Mannes, 1988; Bergfeld-Mills, Diehl, Birkmire and Mou, 1995; Richard, 1990; Schmalhofer and Glavanov, 1986.
2. Schmalhofer and Glavanov, 1986.
3. Pennington, 1987a.
4. Rouet, Deleuze-Dordron and Bisseret, 1995a.
5. Riecken, Koenemann-Belliveau and Robertson, 1991.
6. Littman, Pinto, Letovsky and Soloway, 1986. Koeneman and Robertson, 1991.
7. Pennington, 1987a.
8. Burkhardt, 1997; Burkhardt, Détienne and Wiedenbeck, 1999.
9. Rosson and Carroll, 1993.
10. See, for example, Perrig and Kintsch, 1985.
11. Teasley, 1994.
12. Sheppard, Curtis, Milliman and Love, 1979; Sheppard, Curtis, Milliman, Borst and Love, 1979.
13. Détienne, 1986; Détienne and Soloway, 1990; Norcio, 1982.

14. Robertson, Davis, Okabe and Fitz-Randolph, 1990.
15. Perrig and Kintsch, 1985.
16. Davies, 1994.
17. Wiedenbeck, 1986a; 1986b.
18. Chatel and Détienne, 1994; Rist,1986; 1990.
19. Fix, Wiedenbeck and Scholtz, 1993; Wiedenbeck, Fix and Scholtz, 1993.
20. See, for example, Ehrlich and Johnson-Laird, 1982.
21. Letovsky and Soloway,1986; Soloway, Pinto, Letovsky, Littman and Lampert, 1988.
22. Burkhardt, Détienne and Wiedenbeck, 1999.
23. Dunsmore, Roper, and Wood Object-oriented inspection in the face of delocalization, 2000.
24. Détienne, Rouet, Burkhardt and Deleuze-Dordron, 1996.
25. Letovsky and Soloway, 1986; Soloway, Pinto, Letovsky, Littman and Lampert, 1988.

8. *The Future for Programming Psychology*

In the first part of this chapter we shall discuss the conditions necessary for the ergonomic implications of the work presented in the previous chapters to be really taken on board by the software community. In the second part, we shall summarize the contribution of the research described in this book to the field of cognitive psychology.

8.1 Prospects for the Software Community

The research described in this work has numerous implications for the software community. These implications relate as much to programming languages, programming environments and program documentation as they do to the training and education of programmers. They have been underlined within and at the end of each chapter. We do not wish to repeat them here but rather to discuss the conditions under which a real transfer of expertise between the fields of programming psychology and software development might take place.

8.1.1 Obstacles

At present, the sort of transfer envisaged above is still far away. We believe that there are several different historical reasons why this is so:

1. A mismatch between the problems addressed in the psychology of programming and the perceived problems of software engineering.
2. Failure to take account of problems of usability in software engineering.
3. Lack of a common language.

For a long time, the problems addressed in programming psychology were far removed from the problems with which software engineering was wrestling. Psychological studies of programming continued to use languages like Basic when industrial software engineering was using much more sophisticated languages such as Ada or C. It is noteworthy that very few of the studies described in this book considered programming in COBOL, for many years the most widely used programming language. Nor did they address the so-called fourth generation programming languages. This situation now seems to be changing, as witness the attention given in this book to object-oriented development and reuse. These are problem areas that are at the heart of the present day software engineering landscape.

From another point of view, there is a mismatch between the level of granularity of the problems addressed. Thus, in software engineering, we are concerned with situations in which programmers develop and maintain systems consisting of millions of lines of code. In studies into the psychology of programming, the situations addressed involve, at best, a few hundred lines of code. Such a divergence of scale inevitably makes one wonder whether the results of the studies can be generalized to real situations that are much larger and more complex. Two arguments can be made to support the validity of the generalization.

First, the way to manage a complex situation is often to decompose it into a set of simpler problems. This procedure leads one back eventually to the sort of situations studied in the psychology of programming – after all, once the overall design of a large system has been completed, work is allocated to individual engineers in units that are typically no more than two or three hundred statements in length. Second, empirical studies carried out recently, where developers have been handling millions of lines of code, show results very similar to those obtained in more restricted situations: for example, the cognitive relevance of the distinction between program model and situational model[1] or the use of at-need strategies during maintenance[2].

In recent years, software engineers have paid increasing attention to the need to ensure the usability of the systems they build. For systems to be used by the general public, problems of usability are identified and addressed from the outset. Unfortunately the same attitude has not always been evinced with regard to the systems that software engineers themselves use. Although there are some examples of software engineering environments that have taken usability issues seriously[3], the dominant problems have been perceived as technical rather than as related to the usability of the systems. The introspective approach, which is the common approach in this field, carries the illusion that usability problems are automatically handled: tool developers will use their own experience as the basis for judging the usefulness of the tools they develop. At the other extreme, quantitative data about software development are gathered but are difficult to interpret due to the nature of the performance indicators collected (e.g. the number of lines of code produced per hour). The lack of attention paid to the issue of usability in this field is probably due to the fact that the users are professionals. It is thought, wrongly, that professionals – and software professionals at that – are in a position to master the complexity of the tools they use.

The lack of a common language has, for a long time, been a handicap to real communication. Each community has evolved with its own concepts and its own terminology. This makes access to the scientific output of the community difficult. At this level, training and popularization are needed; we shall return to this point below.

8.1.2 Removing the Obstacles to Effective Transfer

First of all, we hope that this book will have enabled some members of the software engineering community to discover and appreciate the work that has been done in studying the psychology of programming. Indeed, its writing bears witness to an attempt to transfer knowledge to that community. It seems that the software engineering community has recently become more aware of problems of usability. The use of cognitive models of programming activities and studies aimed at evaluating tools is starting to be advocated, witness the very favourable reception given to papers in the field of programming psychology in conferences traditionally limited to software engineering, such as the International Conference on Software Engineering (ICSE) or the International Workshop on Program Comprehension (IWPC), organized by the reverse engineering community.

Bridges need to be built between the two communities at two levels, education and research. Although the ergonomics of user interfaces are frequently studied, few university courses in Computer Science or Software Engineering take any account of the knowledge that we have about the psychology of programming. An attempt to make future software engineers aware of this field ought to equip them with the theoretical and methodological tools needed to tackle problems associated with the usability of software development methods and tools. We do not claim that such an education will enable the software engineer to dispense with the ergonomist in the specification and evaluation of software engineering tools. Rather, it should provide a basis to ensure that future collaboration between ergonomists and psychologists on the one hand, and software engineers on the other, takes place in the best possible conditions.

At the research level, bridges have still to be established through scientific events where the two communities meet each other. Even if workshops such as Empirical Studies of Programmers or the Psychology of Programming Interest Group are already multi-disciplinary, they reach only a small subset of the computing community, and one that is relatively marginalised in comparison with the software engineering community. It seems to us possible to achieve a real strengthening of these exchanges by organizing symposia on the psychology of programming within software engineering conferences. A first step in this direction was taken with the organization of a working session on the cognitive aspects of comprehension at IWPC '98; the themes for the session were taken from a report[4] identifying promising research directions in reverse engineering.

It seems to us that the ideal conditions for transfer of knowledge between the two communities would be found in real research collaborations in designing new software engineering tools. We have personal experience of how enriching this can be for both communities in the development of the CO2 language and environment[5] and in the development of HoodNICE and ReuseNICE[6]. To encourage such collaborations, institutional initiatives are necessary at the level of national and international research programmes. The identification of topics linked to the psychology of programming and to the usability of software engineering tools would promote such research and the effective transfer of its outcomes into software engineering, thus leading that community to recognize its value.

8.2 Contributions to Cognitive Psychology

The theoretical background borrowed from cognitive psychology to handle the design and comprehension of software belongs to the fields of problem solving, analogical reasoning, and text production and comprehension in natural language. These studies of programming deal with activities for which the goal of the task and the level of experience of the subjects are important factors in the situation. They enrich the theoretical foundations of cognitive science and allow their validity in the real world to be evaluated. These theoretical foundations were constructed on the basis of laboratory studies and the role of expertise in a complex domain was often neglected.

So far as design is concerned, the work described illustrates applications of the theory of schemas and also opportunistic models of the design process. It enriches the theoretical foundations in the problem solving area by identifying the conditions under which the various design strategies are employed and opportunistic diversions from the hierarchical design model chosen.

Reuse during design has been studied in the context of models of analogical reasoning. The majority of these models are based on the analysis of artificial laboratory situations in which the source is provided. The study of software reuse has allowed these models, especially that of Clement, to be enriched in several ways: generation processes, understanding, and use of the source. We have also constructed a cognitive classification of reuse situations, which shows that different mechanisms are involved in reuse depending on the development phase of the target.

With regard to program comprehension, we have particularly developed the mental model approach that comes out of research on text comprehension. We have enriched the theoretical foundations by demonstrating the role played by expertise and by the reading objective in program comprehension. One completely original result is the interaction between these two factors and the type of the model constructed: for example, a reuse task tends to diminish the gap between expert and novice so far as the construction of a situational model is concerned, something that is not the case when the task is one of modification.

In this work we have concentrated on design and understanding of programs. One limitation of the work described is that it does not make clearly apparent the links that exist between these activities. The same limitation is also to be found in the theoretical foundations of text production and comprehension. One implicit hypothesis that is made in the studies of programming is that the schematic knowledge used in these two activities is common, while the cognitive processes through which such knowledge is used, as well as the representations constructed, are in part distinct.

To go further, as Heurley (1994) suggests, it is essential to distinguish the notions of blocks of information used in text production, the units into which the text is segmented (such as paragraphs for narrative texts or methods for programs), and the units of analysis (chunks) used during reading. In his studies of the production of natural language text, Heurley suggests that blocks of information constitute processing units in the context of text production. The inter-block positions appear as privileged places for starting revision or global planning activities. These blocks of information appear as textual units made up of one or more propositions organized around the main theme, that is, the principal piece of information, of the block.

8.3 References

1. Von Mayrhauser and Vans, 1998.
2. Singer and Lethbridge, 1998.
3. See, for example, Bott, 1989, Chapters 5 and 6.
4. Tilley, 1998.
5. Carried out in collaboration with GIP Altair. See O. Deux *et al*. 1989.
6. Carried out as part of the ESPRIT 3 project SCALE. See Oquendo, Détienne, Gallo, Kastner and Martelli, 1993.

References

Abelson, R.P. (1981) Psychological status of the script concept. *American Psychologist*, 36(7), 715–729.

Adelson, B. (1981) Problem solving and the development of abstract categories in programming languages. *Memory and Cognition*, 9(4), 422–433.

Adelson, B. (1984) When novices surpass experts: the difficulty of a task may increase with expertise. *Journal of Experimental Psychology: Learning, Memory and Cognition*, 10(3), 483–495.

Adelson, B. (1985) Comparing natural and abstract categories: a case study from computer science. *Cognitive Science*, 9, 417–430.

Adelson, B. and Soloway, E. (1985) The role of domain experience in software design. *IEEE Transactions on Software Engineering*, SE-11, 1351–1360.

Adelson, B. and Soloway, E. (1988) A model of software design. In M.T.H. Chi, R. Glaser and M.J. Farr (eds), *The nature of expertise*, p. 185–208. Laurence Erlbaum Associates Inc., Hillsdale, NJ.

Anderson, J.R., Boyle, C.F., Farrell, R. and Reisner, B.J. (1987) Cognitive principles in the design of computer tutors. In P. Morris (ed.), *Modelling Cognition*. John Wiley, Chichester.

Arblaster, A.T., Sime, M.E. and Green, T.R.G. (1978) Jumping to some purpose. *The Computer Journal*, 22(2), 105–109.

Atwood, M. E. and Ramsey, H. R. (1978) Cognitive structures in the comprehension and memory of computer programs: an investigation of computer program debugging. US Army Research Institute for the Behavioral and Social Sciences, *Technical Report* (TR-78-A21). Alexandra, VA.

Batra, D. and Davis, J.G. (1992) Conceptual data modelling in database design: similarities and differences between expert and novice designers. *International Journal of Man-Machine Studies*, 37, 83–101.

Baudet, S. and Cordier, F. (1995) Une procédure d'action complexe. Etude comparative d'une organisation fondée sur les objets versus les actions. Presses Universitaires de Reims, Hommage à Geneviève Hily-Mane.

Bellamy, R.K.E. (1994a) What does pseudo-code do? A psychological analysis of the use of pseudo-code by experienced programmers. *Human-Computer Interaction*, 9, 225–246.

Bellamy, R.K.E. (1994b) Strategy analysis: an approach to psychological analysis of artefacts, in D.J. Gilmore, R.L. Winder, and F. Détienne (eds), *User-Centred Requirements for Software Engineering Environments*, pp. 57–68. Springer-Verlag, Berlin.

Bereiter, C. Burtis, P.J. and Scardamalia, M. (1988). Cognitive operations in constructing main points in written composition. *Journal of Memory and Language*, 27, 261–278.

Bergfeld-Mills, C., Dhiel, V.A., Birkmire, D. P. and Mou, L. C. (1993) Procedural text: predictions of importance ratings and recall by models of reading comprehension. *Discourse Processes*, 16(3), 279–315.

Bergfeld-Mills, C., Dhiel, V.A., Birkmire, D.P. and Mou, L.C. (1995) Reading procedural texts: effects of purpose for reading and predictions of reading comprehension models. *Discourse Processes*, 20, 79–107.

Biggerstaff, T.J. and Perlis, A.J. (ed.) (1989) *Software reusability: concepts and models*. New York ACM Press, New York.

Bisseret, A., Burkhardt, J-M., Deleuze-Dordron, C., Détienne, F., Rouet, J-F. (1995) The role of software structuration and documentation formats in software reuse: result of advanced studies. SCALE European project. Deliverable 2.3.2–3.

Black, J.B., Kay, D.S. and Soloway, E. (1986) Goal and Plan Knowledge Representations: From Stories to Text Editors and Programs. In Carroll, J.M. (ed.), *Interfacing Thought: Cognitive Aspects of Human-Computer Interaction*. MIT Press, Cambridge, MA.

Böcker, H-D. and Herczeg, J. (1990) Browsing through program execution, in D. Diaper, D. Gilmore, G. Cockton and B. Shacker (eds), *Human Computer Interaction*, Proceedings of INTERACT '90, pp. 991–996, North Holland.

Boehm-Davis, D.A. and Ross, L.S. (1992) Program design methodologies and the software development process. *International Journal of Man-Machine Studies*, 36, 1–19.

Boehm-Davis, D.A. Holt, R.W. and Schultz, A.C. (1992). The role of program structure in software maintenenace. *International Journal of Man-Machine Studies*, 36, 21–63.

Bonar, J. and Cunningham, R. (1988) Bridge: an intelligent tutor for thinking about programming, in J. Self (ed.), *Artificial intelligence and human learning*. Chapman and Hall. London.

Borgida, A., Greenspan, S. and Mylopoulos, J. (1986) Knowledge representations as the basis for requirements specifications, in C. Rich and R.C. Waters (eds), *Readings in Artificial Intelligence and Software Engineering*, p. 561–570. Morgan Kaufmann, Palo Alto, CA.

Bott, M.F. (ed.) (1989) *Eclipse: An Integrated Project Support Environment*, p. 245. Peter Peregrinus, London.

Bower, G.H., Black, J.B. and Turner, T. J. (1979) Scripts in memory for text. *Cognitive Psychology*, 11, 177–220.

Brangier, E. and Bobiller-Chaumon, M-E. (1995) Approche psycho-ergonomique comparée de l'utilisation d'environnements de programmation procédural et orienté-objets. Actes du congrès AFCET'95.

Brooks, R. (1977) Towards a theory of the cognitive processes in computer programming. *International Journal of Man-Machine Studies*, 9, 737–751.

Brooks, R. (1980) Studying programmers behavior experimentally: the problems of proper methodology. *Communications of the ACM*, 23(4), 207–213.

Brooks, R. (1983) Towards a Theory of the Comprehension of Computer Programs. *International Journal of Man-Machine Studies*, 18, 543–554.

Burkhardt, J-M. (1997) Réutilisation en conception orienté-objet: analyse des représentations et processus cognitifs. Thèse de Doctorat, Université Paris 5.

Burkhardt, J.-M. and Détienne, F. (1994). La réutilisation en génie logiciel: une définition d'un cadre théorique en ergonomie cognitive, in *ERGO.IA '94*, pp. 83–95, 26–28 octobre, Biarritz, I.D.L.S.

Burkhardt, J-M. and Détienne, F. (1995a) La réutilisation de solutions en conception de programmes informatiques, *Psychologie Française*, 40-1, 85–98.

Burkhardt, J-M., and Détienne, F. (1995b) An empirical study of software reuse by experts in object-oriented design, in K. Nordby, P.H. Helmersen, D.J. Gilmore and Arnesen, S.A. (eds), *Human Computer Interaction*, Proceedings of INTERACT '95, pp. 133–138, Chapman and Hall, London.

Burkhardt, J-M., Détienne, F. and Wiedenbeck, S. (1997) Mental representations constructed by experts and novices in object-oriented comprehension. In S. Howard, J. Hammond and G. Lingaard (eds), *Human-Computer Interaction*: INTERACT '97, Chapman and Hall, London.

Burkhardt, J.-M., Détienne, F. and Wiedenbeck, S. (1999) Domain Knowledge and Purpose for Reading: Interacting Factors in Comprehension? The Annual Meeting of the Society for Text and Discourse, 15–17 August 1999, Vancouver, Canada.

Bürkle, U., Gryczan, G. and Züllighoven, H. (1995) Object-Oriented System Development in a Banking Project: Methodology, Experience, and Conclusions. *Human-Computer Interaction*, 10(2 and 3), 293–336.

Carroll, J.M., Thomas, J.C. and Malhotra, A. (1979) Clinical-experimental analysis of design problem solving. *Design Studies*, 1, 84–92.

Chase, W.G. and Simon, H.A. (1973) Perception in chess. *Cognitive Psychology*, 4, 55–81.

Chatel, S. and Détienne. F. (1996) Strategies in object-oriented design. *Acta Psychologica*, 91, 245–269.

Chatel, S. (1997) L'apprentissage d'un langage de programmation orienté-objet, Smalltalk_80. Thèse de Doctorat, Université Paris 8.

Chatel, S. and Détienne, F. (1994) Expertise in Object-Oriented Programming. Proceedings of ECCE7, 5–8 Septembre. Bonn.

Chatel, S., Détienne, F. and Borne, I. (1992) Transfer among programming languages: an assessment of various indicators. In F. Détienne (ed.) *Proceedings of the Fifth Workshop of the Psychology of Programming Interest Group*, 10– 12 September, pp. 261–272, Paris, France.

Chi, M.T.H., Feltovitch, P.J. and Glaser, R. (1981) Categorization and representation of physics problems by experts and novices. *Cognitive Science*, 5, 121–152.

Chomsky, N. (1965) *Aspects of the Theory of Syntax*. MIT Press, Cambridge, MA.

Clement, J. (1981) Analogy generation in scientific problem solving. *Proceedings of the Third Annual Conference of the Cognitive Science Society*, 2, 137–140.

Clement, J. (1986) Methods for evaluating the validity of hypothesized analogies, Proceedings of the Eight Annual Conference of the Cognitive Science Society. Lawrence Erlbaum Associates Inc., Hillsdale, NJ.

Clement, J. (1988) Observed methods for generating analogies in scientific problem solving. *Cognitive Science*, 12, 563–586.

Cointe, P. (1986) Une introduction à la Programmation par Objet. 2ème Journées Base de Données Avancées, Giens 86.

Curtis, B. (1980) Measurement and experimentation. *Proceedings of the IEEE*, 68(9), 1144–1157.

Curtis, B. (1982) A review of human factors research on programming languages and specifications. *Human Factors in Computer System*, 15-(17), 212–218.

Curtis, B. (1984) Fifteen years of psychology in software engineering: individual differences and cognitive science. Proceeding of the Seventh Conference on Software Engineering, 26–29 Marsh, Orlando, Florida, USA.

Curtis, B. (1986) By the Way, Did Anyone Study Any Real Programmers? in E. Soloway and S. Iyengar (eds), *Empirical Studies of Programmers, First Workshop*, pp. 256–262. Ablex Publishing Corporation, Norwood, NJ.

Curtis, B., Forman, I., Brooks, R., Soloway, E. and Ehrlich, K. (1984)/ Psychological perspectives for software science. *Information Processing and Management*, 20(12), 81–96.

Curtis, B., Krasner, H. and Iscoe, N. (1988) A field study of the software design process for large systems. *Communications of the ACM*, 31, 1268–1287.

Curtis, B. and Walz, D. (1990) The psychology of programming in the large: team and organizational behavior, in J-M. Hoc, T.R.G. Green, R. Samurcay and D. Gilmore (eds), *Psychology of Programming*, pp. 253–270. Academic Press, London.

D'Alessandro, M. and Martelli, A. (1994) ReuseNICE: a toolset to nicely support reuse, in Proc. XIV International Conference of the Chilean Computer Science Society, Oct 31- Nov 4, 1994. Conception, Chile.

Dahl, O.J., Dijkstra, E. and Hoare, C.A.R. (1972) *Structured programming*. Academic Press, Orlando/ London.

Daly, J., Brooks, A., Miller, J., Roper, M. and Wood, M. (1996) Evaluating the effect of inheritance on the maintainability of object-oriented software, in W. Gray and D. A. Boehm-Davis (eds), *Empirical Studies of Programmers, Sixth Workshop*, 5-7 January 1996. Washington DC, US.

Darses, F. (1992). Mécanismes cognitifs de gestion de contraintes dans la résolution de problèmes de conception, in Actes de Ergo.IA 92. Biarritz: IDLS.

D'Astous, P. Détienne, F. Robillard, P. N. and Visser, W. (1997) Technical review meetings: a framework for cognitive analysis. Poster: Seventh Workshop on Empirical Studies of Programmers (ESP7), 24–26 October. Washington DC.

D'Astous, P., Détienne, F., Robillard, P. N. and Visser, W. (1998) A coding scheme to analyse activities in Technical Review Meetings. The 10th Workshop of the Psychology of Programming Interest Group (PPIG98), 5-7 January. Milton Keynes, UK.

Davies, S. P. (1990a) Plans, goals and selection rules in the comprehension of computer programs. *Behaviour and Information Technology*, 9, 201–214.

Davies, S. P. (1990b) The nature and development of programming plans. *International Journal of Man-Machine Studies*, 18, 543–554.

Davies, S. P. (1991) The role of notation and knowledge reprresentation in the determination of programming strategy: a framework for integrating models of programming behavior. *Cognitive Science*, 15, 547–572.

Davies, S. P. (1993a) Models and theories of programming strategy. *International Journal of Man-Machine Studies*, 39, 237–267.

Davies, S. P. (1993b) The structure and content of programming knowledge: disentangling training and language effects in theories of skill development. *International Journal of Human-Computer Interaction*, 5(4), 325–346.

Davies, S. P. (1994) Knowledge restructuring and the acquisition of programming expertise. *International Journal of Human-Computer Studies*, 40, 703–726.

Davies, S. (1996) Display-based problem solving strategies in computer programming, in W.D. Gray and D.A. Boehm-Davis (eds), *Empirical studies of programmers, sixth workshop*, pp. 59–76, Ablex Publishing Corporation, Norwood, NJ.

Davies, S. P., and Castell, A. M. (1994) From individual to groups through artifacts: the changing semantics of design in software development, in D. Gilmore, R. Winder and F. Détienne (eds), *User Centred Requirements for Software Engineering Environments*, pp. 11–23. Springer Verlag, NATO ASI Series.

Davies, S.P., Gilmore, D.J., and Green, T.R.G. (1995) Are Objects That Important? The Effects of Familiarity and Expertise on the Classification of Object-Oriented Code. *Human-Computer Interaction*, 10 (2 and 3), 227–249.

Denhière, G. (1985) Statut psychologique du paragraphe et structure du récit, in J. Chatillon (ed.) *La notion de paragraphe*, pp. 121–128. Ed. du CNRS, Paris.

Détienne, F. (1984) Analyse exploratoire de l'activité de compréhension des programmes informatiques. Proceeding AFCET, séminaire "Approches Quantitatives en Génie Logiciel", 7–8 Juin. Sophia-Antipolis, France.

Détienne, F. (1986) La compréhension de programmes informatiques par l'expert: un modèle en termes de schémas. Thèse de doctorat. Université Paris V. *Sciences humaines*, Sorbonne, 1986.

Détienne, F. (1990a) Difficulties in Designing with an object-oriented language: an empirical study. In: D. Diaper, D. Gilmore, G. Cockton and B. Shacker (eds), *Human Computer Interaction*, pp. 971–976, Proceedings of INTERACT'90. North Holland.

Détienne, F. (1990b) Program Understanding and Knowledge Organization: the Influence of Acquired Schemas, in P. Falzon (ed) *Cognitive Ergonomics: Understanding, Learning and Designing Human-Computer Interaction*, pp. 245–256. Academic Press, London.

Détienne, F. (1990c) Expert Programming Knowledge: A Schema-Based Approach, in J-M. Hoc, T.R.G. Green, R. Samurçay, D. Gilmore (eds), *Psychology of Programming*, pp. 205–222. People and Computer Series. Academic Press.

Détienne, F. (1990d) Un exemple d'évaluation ergonomique d'un système de programmation orienté-objet, le système O2. Actes du congrès ERGO.IA'90, 19–21 Septembre, Biarritz.

Détienne, F. (1991) Reasoning from a schema and from an analog in software code reuse, in J. Koenemann-Belliveau, T. Moher, and S.P. Robertson (eds), *Empirical studies of programmers, fourth workshop*, Ablex Publishing Corporation, Norwood, NJ.

Détienne, F. (1995) Design strategies and knowledge in object-oriented programming: effects of experience. *Human-Computer Interaction*, 10(2 and 3), 129–170.

Détienne, F. (1997) Assessing the cognitive consequences of the object-oriented approach: a survey of empirical research on object-oriented design by individuals and teams. *Interacting with Computers*, 9, 47–72.

Détienne, F., and Rist. R. (1995) Introduction to this special issue on Empirical Studies of Object-Oriented Design. *Human-Computer Interaction*, Vol. 10(2 and 3), 121–128.

Détienne, F., Rouet, J-F., Burkhardt, J-M. and Deleuze-Dordron, C. (1996) Reusing processes and documenting processes: toward an integrated framework. Proceedings of the Eighth Conference on Cognitive Ergonomics (ECCE8), 10–13 September. Grenada, Spain.

Détienne, F. and Soloway, E. (1990) An Empirically-Derived Control Structure for the Process of Program Understanding, in R. Brooks (Ed) Special issue: "What Programmers Know", *International Journal of Man-Machine Studies*, 33(3), 323–342.

Deux O. et al. (1989) The story of O2. Rapport technique 37–89, GIP Altaïr.

De Vries, E. (1993). The role of case-based reasoning in architectural design: Stretching the design problem space. In W. Visser (ed.) Proceedings of the Workshop of the Thirteenth International Joint Conference on Artificial Intelligence "Reuse of designs : an interdisciplinary cognitive approach", pp. B1-B13, 29 August 1993: INRIA Rocquencourt, Chambery.

Dunsmore, A., Roper, M. and Wood, M. Object-oriented inspection in the face of delocalisation. *Proceedings ICSE 2000*, pp. 467–476. ACM Press, New York

Dvorak, J. (1994) Conceptual entropy and its effect on class hierarchies. *IEEE Computer*, 27(6), 59–63.

Dvorak, J.L., and Moher, T.G. (1991) A feasability study of early class hierarchy construction in object-oriented development, in J. Koenemann-Belliveau, T. G. Moher and S. P. Robertson (eds), Empirical Studies of Programmers, Fourth Workshop, pp. 23–35. Ablex, Norwood, NJ.

Ehrlich, K. and Johnson-Laird, P.N. (1982) Spatial description and referential continuity. *Journal of Verbal Learning and Verbal Behavior*, 21, 296–306.

Ehrlich, M-F., Tardieu, H. and Cavazza, M. (1993) *Les Modèles Mentaux: Approche Cognitive des Représentations*. Masson, Paris.

Ericsson, K.A. and Simon, H.A. (1980) Verbal reports as data. *Psychological Review*, 87(3), 215–251.

Eteläpelto, A. (1993) Metacognition and the expertise of computer program comprehension. *Scandinavian Journal of Educational Research*, 37, 243–254.

Fischer, G., Henninger, S. and Redmiles, D. (1991) Cognitive Tools for Locating and Comprehending Software Objects for Reuse. *Proceedings of the 13th Conference on Software Engineering*, pp. 318–328.

Fischer, G. and Nieper-Lemke, H. (1989) HELGON: Extending the Retrieval by Reformulation Paradigm, CHI'89 Proceedings, pp. 357–362.

Fischer, G., Redmiles, D., Williams, L., Puhr, G., Aoki, A. and Nakakoji, K. (1995) Beyond object-oriented development: Where current object-oriented approaches fall short. *Human-Computer Interaction*, 10, 79–199.

Fix, V. and Wiedenbeck, S. (1996) An intelligent tool to aid students in learning second and subsequent programming languages. *Computers Education*, 27(2), 71–83.

Fix, V., Wiedenbeck, S. and Scholtz, J. (1993) Mental representations of programs by novices and experts. *Proceedings of INTERCHI'93*, pp. 74–79.

Florès, C. (1970) Mémoire à court terme terme et à long terme, in: *La Mémoire*, PUF, Paris.

Galambos, J.A., Abelson, R.P., and Black, J.B. (1986) *Knowledge Structures*. Laurence Erlbaum Associates INC., Hillsdale, NJ.

Gamma, E., Helm, R. Johnson, R., and Vlissides, J. (1994) *Design patterns, elements of reusable object-oriented software*. Addison-Wesley professional computing series.

Gannon, J. D. (1976) An experiment for the evaluation of language features. *International Journal of Man-Machine Studies*, 8, 61–73.

Gannon, J. D. (1977) An experimental evaluation of data type convention. *Communication of ACM*, 20 (8), 584–599.

Gentner, D. (1983) Structure-mapping: a theoretical framework for analogy. *Cognitive Science*, 7, 155–170.

Gentner, D. (1989) The mechanisms of analogical learning, in S. Vosniadou and A. Ortny (eds), *Similarity and Analogical Reasoning*, pp. 199–241. Cambridge University Press, New York.

Gick, M.L. and Holyoak, K.J. (1983) Schema induction and analogical tranfer. *Cognitive Psychology*, 15, 1–38.

Gilmore, D. J. (1990) Expert programming knowledge: a strategic approach, in J-M. Hoc, T.R.G. Green, R. Samurçay, D. Gilmore (eds), Psychology of programming, pp. 223–234. People and Computer Series.

Gilmore, D.J. and Green, T.R.G. (1984a) The comprehensibility of programming notations. Proceedings of the Congress Interact, September 1984 London, England.

Gilmore, D.J. and Green, T.R.G. (1984b) Comprehension and recall of miniature programs. *International Journal of Man-Machine Studies*, 21, 31–48.

Gilmore, D.J. and Smith, H.T. (1984) An investigation of the utility of flowcharts during computer program debugging. *International Journal of Man-Machine Studies*, 20, 357–372.

Gray, W.D. and Anderson, J.R. (1987) Change-episode in coding: when and how programmers change their code? in G. M. Olson, S. Sheppard and E. Soloway (eds), *Empirical studies of programmers, second workshop*. pp. 185–197. Ablex Publishing Corporation, Norwood, NJ.

Green, T.R.G. (1989) Cognitive dimensions of notations, in A. Sutcliffe and L. Macaulay (eds), *People and Computers*, V. Cambridge University Press, Cambridge.

Green, T.R.G. (1990) Programming languages as information structures, in J-M Hoc, T.R.G. Green, R. Samurçay and D. Gilmore (eds), *Psychology of Programming*, pp. 117–138. Série Cognitive Ergonomics and Cognitive Engineering, Academic Press, London.

Green, T.R.G., Bellamy, R.K.E. and Parker, M. (1987). Parsing and Gnisrap : a model of device use, in G. Olson, S. Sheppard and E. Soloway (eds), *Empirical Studies of Programmers: Second Workshop*, pp. 132–146. Ablex Publishing Corporation, Norwood, NJ.

Green, T.R.G., Gilmore, D. J., Blumenthal, B. B., Davies, S. and Winder, R. (1992) Towards a Cognitive Browser for OOPS. *International Journal of Human-Computer Interaction*, 4, 1–34.

Green, T.R.G., and Petre, M. (1996) Usability analysis of visual programming environments: a 'cognitive dimensions' framework. *Journal of Visual Languages and Computing*, 7, 131–174.

Guindon, R. (1990a) Designing the design process: exploiting opportunistic thoughts. *Human-Computer Interaction*, 5, 305–344.

Guindon, R. (1990b) Knowledge exploited by experts during software system design. *International Journal of Man-Machine Studies*, 33(3), 279–304.

Guindon, R. (1992) Requirements and design of Design Vision, an object-oriented graphical interface to an intelligent software design assistant. In *Proceedings of CHI'92*, pp. 499–506. ACM Press, New York.

Guindon, R. and Curtis, B. (1988) Control of cognitive processes during design: what tools are needed? In *Proceedings of CHI '88*, ACM, New York.

Guindon, R. Krasner, H. and Curtis, B. (1987) Breakdowns and Processes during the Early Activities of Software Design by Professionals, in G.M. Olson, S. Sheppard and E. Soloway (eds), *Empirical Studies of Programmers: Second Workshop*. Ablex.

Guyard, J. and Jacquot, J.P. (1984) MAIDAY: an environment for guided programming with a definitional language. 7th International Conference on Software Engineering, Orlando, USA.

Haberlandt, K. and Graesser, A. (1985) Component processes in text comprehension and some of their interactions. *Journal of Experimental Psychology: General*, 114, 357–374.

Halstead, M. H. (1977) *Elements for Software Science*. Elsevier North-Holland, New York.

Hayes, J.R. and Flower, L. (1980). Identifying the organization of writing processes, in L.W. Gregg and E. Steinberg (eds), *Cognitive processes in writing*, pp. 3–30. Laurence Erlbaum Associates INC., Hillsdale, NJ.

Henry, D., Green, T.R.G., Gilmore, D. and Davies, S. (1992) Improving the communicability of spreadsheet designs: annotating with descriptive tags, in F. Détienne (ed): *Proceedings of the fifth workshop of the psychology of programming interest group*, pp. 91–93, 10–12 December 1992, Paris, France.

Henry, S. and Humphrey, M. (1993). Object-oriented vs. procedural programming languages: Effectiveness in program maintenance. *Journal of Object-Oriented Programming*, 6(3), 41–49.

Herbsleb, J. D., Klein, H., Olson, G. M., Brunner, H., Olson, J. S. and Harding, J. (1995) Object-oriented analysis and design in software project teams. *Human-Computer Interaction*, 10 (2and 3), 249–292.

Heurley, L. (1994) Traitement de textes procéduraux: étude de psycholinguistique cognitive des processus de production et de compréhension chez des adultes non experts. Thèse de doctorat de l'Université de Bourgogne.

Hoc, J-M. (1981) Planning and Direction of Problem-Solving in Structured Programming: an Empirical Comparaison between two methods. *International Journal of Man-Machine Studies*, 15(4), 363–383.

Hoc, J-M. (1982a) L'étude psychologique de l'activité de programmation: une revue de question. *Technique et Sciences Informatiques*, 1 (5), 383–392.

Hoc, J-M. (1982b) Psychologie cognitive et génie logiciel. *Intellectica*, 1 (1), 21–36.

Hoc, J-M. (1983) Une méthode de classification préalable des problèmes d'un domaine pour l'analyse des stratégies de résolution: la programmation informatique chez des professionnels. *Le Travail Humain*, 46 (3), 205–217.

Hoc, J-M. (1984a) La verbalisation provoquée pour l'étude du fonctionnement cognitif. *Psychologie Française*, 29 (3–4), 231–234.

Hoc, J.-M. (1984b). Les activités de résolution de problème dans la programmation informatique. *Psychologie Française*, 29(3–4), 267–271.

Hoc, J-M. (1987a) L'apprentissage de l'utilisation des dispositifs informatiques par analogie à des situations familières. *Psychologie Française*, Numéro spécial: Les langages informatiques dans l'enseignement, 32(4), 217–226.

Hoc, J-M. (1987b) Psychologie cognitive de la planification. PUG, Collection *Sciences et Technologies de la Connaissance*.

Hoc, J-M. (1988) Towards effective computer aids to planning in computer programming. Theoretical concern and empirical evidence drawn from assessment of a prototype, in G.C. van der Veer, T.R.G. Green, J-M. Hoc, and D. Murray (eds), *Working with computers, theory versus outcomes*. Academic Press, London.

Hoc, J.-M., Green, T.R.G., Samurçay, R. and Gilmore, D. (eds), (1990) *Psychology of Programming*. Academic Press, London

Hoc, J-M. and Leplat, J. (1983) Evaluation of different modalities of verbalization in a sorting task. *International Journal of Man-Machine Studies*, 18, 283–306.

Hoc, J-M, and Nguyen-Xuan, A. (1990) Language semantics, mental models and analogy, in J-M. Hoc, T.R.G. Green, R. Samurçay, and D.J. Gilmore (eds), *Psychology of Programming*, pp. 139–156. Computer and People Series, Academic Press, London.

Holyak, K. J. (1985) The pragmatics of analogical tranfer, in G. H. Bower (ed) *The Psychology of Learning and Motivation*, Vol. 19, pp. 59–87. Academic Press, New York.

ICSE (2000) 2000 International Conference on Software Engineering, Limerick, Ireland. Association for Computing Machinery, New York.

Jeffries, R., Turner, A.A., Polson, P. and Atwood, M.E. (1981) The Processes Involved in Designing Software, in J.R. Anderson (ed) *Cognitive Skills and Their Acquisition*. Laurence Erlbaum Associates INC., Hillside, NJ.

Johnson-Laird, P. N. (1983) *Mental Models*. Cambridge University Press, Cambridge.

Kamath, Y.H. and Smith, J.G. (1992). Experiences in C++. *JOOP*, November-December 1992, pp. 23–28.

Kant, E. and Newell, A. (1984) Problem solving techniques for the design of algorithms. *Information Processing and Management*, 20, 97–118.

Karsenty, L. (1996) An empirical evaluation of design rationale documents, in M.J. Tauber, V. Belloti, R. Jeffries, J.D. Mackinlay and J. Nielsen (eds): *CHI '96 Conference Proceedings*, pp. 150–156. ACM Press, New York.

Kim, J. and J. Lerch (1992) Towards a model of cognitive process in logical design: comparing object-oriented and traditionnal functional decomposition software methodologies, in P. Bauersfeld, J. Bennett and G. Lynch (eds), *Proceedings of CHI '92 Conference on Human Factors in Computing Systems*, ACM Press, New York.

Kintsch, W. (1974) *The representation of meaning in memory*. Laurence Erlbaum Associates INC., Hillsdale, NJ.

Kintsch, W. (1988) The role of knowledge in discourse comprehension: a construction-integration model. *Psychological Review*, 95, 2, 163–182.

Kintsch, W. (1992) A cognitive architecture for comprehension, in H.L. Pick, P. van den Brock and D.C. Knill (eds), *The Study of Cognition: Conceptual and Methodological Issues*, pp. 143–163. American Psychological Association, Washington DC:

Kintsch, W. (1994) Text comprehension, memory and learning. *American Psychologist*, 49(4), 294–303.

Kintsch, W., and Keenan, J. M. (1973) Reading rate and retention as a function of the number of propositions in the base structure of sentences. *Cognitive Psychology*, 5, 257–374.

Kintsch, W. and Van Dijk, T. (1978) Toward a model of text comprehension and production. *Psychological Review*, 85, 363- 394.

Koenemann, J. and Robertson, S.P. (1991) Expert Problem Solving Strategies for program Comprehension, in S.P. Robertson, G. M. Olson and J. S. Olson (eds), *CHI'91 Conference Proceedings*, pp. 125–130.

Krasner, H., Curtis, B. and Iscoe, N. (1987) Communication breakdowns and boundary spanning activities on large programming projects, in G.M. Olson, S. Sheppard and E. Soloway (eds), *Empirical Studies of Programmers: Second Workshop*, pp. 47–64. Ablex.

Lange, B.M. and Moher T.G. (1989) Some strategies of reuse in an object-oriented programming environment, in K. Bice and C. Lewis (eds), *Proceedings of CHI '89 Conference on Human Factors in Computing Systems*, pp. 69–73. ACM Press, New York.

Laughery, K.R. and Laughery, K.R. (1985) Human Factors in Software Engineering: a review of the Literature. *The Journal of Systems and Software*, 5, 3–14.

Lee, A. and Pennington, N. (1994) The effects of programming on cognitive activities in design. *International Journal of Human-Computer Studies*, 40, 577–601.

Leplat, J. and Paillhous, J. (1977) La description de la tâche: statut et rôle dans la résolution de problème. *Bulletin de Psychologie*, 332, XXXI, 149–156.

Leplat, J. and Hoc, J-M. (1983) Tâche et activité dans l'analyse psychologique des situations. *Cahier de Psychologie Cognitive*, 3 (1), 49–63.

Letovsky, S. and Soloway, E. (1986) Delocalized Plans and Program Comprehension. *IEEE Software*, 3 (3), 1986, 41–49.

Lewis, J.A., Henry, S.M., Kafura D.G. and Schulman, R.S. (1991) An empirical study of the object-oriented paradigm and software reuse. *Proceedings of Object-Oriented Programming, Systems and Applications*, pp. 184–196. ACM Press: New York.

Littman, D.C., Pinto, J., Letovsky, S. and Soloway, E. (1986) Mental Models and Software Maintenance, in E. Soloway and S. Iyengar (eds), *Empirical Studies of Programmers, First Workshop*, pp. 80–98. Ablex Publishing Corporation, Norwood, NJ.

Mandler, J. M. and Johnson, N.S. (1977) Remembrance of things parsed: story structure and recall. *Cognitive Psychology*, 9, 111–151.

Mannes, S. (1988). A theoretical interpretation of learning vs memorizing texts. *European Journal of Psychology of Education*, 3, 157–162.

Mayer, R. (1981) The pychology of how novices learn computer programming. *ACM Computing Surveys*, 13(1), 121–141.

Mayer, R. E. (1987) Cognitive aspects of learning and using a programming language, in J. M. Carroll (ed.) *Interfacing thought: cognitive aspects of human-computer interaction*. MIT Press, Cambridge, MA.

McCabe, T. J. (1976) A complexity measure. *IEEE Transactions on Software Engineering*, SE-2 (4), 308–320.

McIlroy, D. (1969) Mass Produced Software Components, in: J.N. Buxton and B.E. Randell (eds), *Proceedings of the 1968 NATO Conference on Software Engineering*. Scientific Affairs Division, NATO, Brussels.

McKeithen, K. B., Reitman, J. S., Reuter, H. H., and Hirtle, S. C. (1981) Knowledge organization and skill differences in computer programmers. *Cognitive Psychology*, 13, 307–325.

Meyer, B. J. F. (1975) *The organization of prose and its effect upon memory*. North-Holland, Amsterdam.

Meyer, B. (1988) *Object-Oriented Software Construction*. International Series in Computer Science, Prentice Hall,

Mili, H., Mili, F. and Mili, A. (1995) Reusing Software: Issues and Research Directions. *IEEE Transactions on Software Engineering*, 21(6), 528–562

Miller, G. A. (1956) The magical number seven plus or minus two: some limits on our capacity for processing information. *Psychological Review*, 63 , 81–97.

Moher, T. and Schneider, G.M. (1982) Methodology and experimental research in software engineering. International *Journal of Man-Machine Studies*, 16, 65–87.

Moran, T.P. and Carroll, J.M. (1996) Design Rationale: Concepts, Techniques and Uses. Laurence Erlbaum Associates INC., Hillsdale, NJ.

Newell, A. and Simon, H. A. (1972) *Human Problem Solving*. New York: Prentice-Hall.

Norcio, A.F. (1982) Indentation, documentation and program comprehension. *Human Factors in Computing Systems*, 15–17, 118–120.

Norman, D.A. and Bobrow, D.G. (1979) Descriptions: An Intermediate Stage in Memory retrieval. *Cognitive Psychology*, 11, 107–123.

Norman, D.A. and Rumelhart, D.E. (1975) *Explorations in Cognition*. W.H. Freeman, San Francisco, CA.

Oquendo, F., Détienne, F., Gallo, N., Kastner, A. and Martelli, A. (1993) SCALE: Building PCTE-based Process-centred Environments for Large and Fine Grain Reuse. Proceedings of PCTE'93, 17–18 Novembre 1993, Paris, France.

Pair, C. (1990) Programming, programming languages and programming methods, in J.-M. Hoc, T.R.G. Green, R. Samurçay and D. Gilmore (eds), *Psychology of Programming*, pp. 9–19. Academic Press.

Pennington, N. (1987a) Stimulus structures and mental representation in expert comprehension of computer programs. *Cognitive Psychology*, 19, 295–341.

Pennington, N. and Grabowski, B. (1990). The Tasks of Programming, in J.-M. Hoc, T. R. G. Green, R. Samurçay and D. Gilmore (eds), *Psychology of Programming* (pp. 145–162). Academic Press.

Pennington, N., Lee, A. and Rehder, B. (1995) Cognitive activities and levels of abstraction in procedural and object-oriented design. *Human-Computer Interaction*, 10 (2 and 3), 171–226.

Perrig, W. and Kintsch, W. (1985) Propositionnal and situational representations of text. *Journal of Memory and Language*, 24, 503–518.

Petre, M. (1990) Expert programmers and programming languages, in J-M. Hoc, T.R.G. Green, R. Samurçay, D. Gilmore (eds), *Psychology of Programming*, pp. 103–116. People and Computer Series, Academic Press, London.

Petre, M. (1995) Why looking isn't always seeing: readership skills and graphical programming. *Communication of the ACM* (June 1995), pp. 33–44.

Petre, M., and Green, T.R.G. (1992) Requirements for graphical notations for professional users: electronics CAD systems as a case study. *Le Travail Humain*, 55(1), 47–70.

Petre, M. and Green, T.R.G. (1993) Learning to read graphics: some evidence that 'Seeing an information display is an acquired skill'. *Journal of Visual Languages and Computing*, 4, 55–70.

Puglielli, A. (1990) Instructions for use: from macro to micro linguistic analysis, in M. A.K. Halliday, J. Gibbons and H. Nicholas (eds), Learning, keeping and using language, Vol. 2, pp. 315–332. John Benjamins Publishing Company, Amsterdam, Philadelphia.

Rasmussen, J. and Lind, M. (1982) A model of human decision making in complex systems and its use for design of sytem control strategies. Roskilde, Danemark, RISO, M-2349.

Richard, J-F. (1990) Les activités mentales: comprendre, raisonner, trouver des solutions. Armand Colin.

Richard, J-F. (1996) La représentation mentale d'un dispositif du point de vue de son utilisation et de son fonctionnement. Workshop: *Les Sciences Cognitives et le Conception des Systèmes Informatiques*, 26–27 February 1996, Florianopolis, Brasil.

Richard, J-F., Bonnet, C. and Ghiglione, R. (1990) Traité de Psychologie Cognitive 2, Le traitement de l'information symbolique. Dunod, Paris.

Riecken, R.D., Koenemann-Belliveau, J. and Robertson, S.P. (1991) What do expert programmers communicate by means of descriptive commenting? in J. Koenemann-Belliveau, T.G. Moher and S.P. Robtertson (eds), *Empirical Studies of Programmers, Fourth Workshop*, pp. 177–193. Ablex Publishing Corporation, Norwood, NJ.

Rist, R. (1986) Plans in Programming: Definition, Demonstration, and Development, in E. Soloway and S. Iyengar (eds), *Empirical Studies of Programmers*: First Workshop. Ablex Publishing Corporation, Norwood, NJ.

Rist, R. S. (1989) Schema creation in programming. *Cognitive Science*, 13, 389–414.

Rist, R. S. (1990) Variability in program design: the interaction of process with knowledge. *International Journal of Man-Machine Studies*, 33 (3), 305–322.

Rist, R. S. (1991) Knowledge creation and retrieval in program design: a comparison of novice and experienced programmers. *Human-Computer Interaction*, 6, 1–46.

Rist, R. S. (1995) Program structure and design. *Cognitive Science*, 19, 507–562.

Rist, R. S. (1996) System structure and design, in W.D. Gray and D.A. Boehm-Davis (eds), *Empirical Studies of Programmers, Sixth Workshop*, pp. 163–194. Ablex Publishing Corporation, Norwood: NJ.

Rist, R. S. and Terwilliger, R. (1995) *Object-oriented design in Eiffel*. Prentice Hall, Sydney.

Robertson, S. P. (1990) Knowledge Representations used by Computer Programmers. *Journal of the Washington Academy of Sciences*, 80(3), pp. 116–137.

Robertson, S.P., Davis, E.F., Okabe, K. and Fitz-Randolf, D. (1990) Program Comprehension Beyond the Line, in D. Diaper *et al.* (eds), Human-Computer Interaction, *Proceedings of INTERACT '90*. pp. 959–963. Elsevier Science Publishers: North Holland.

Robertson, S.R. and Yu, C-C. (1990) Common cognitive representations of program code across tasks and languages. *International Journal of Man-Machine Studies*, 33, pp. 343–360.

Robillard, P. N., D'Astous, P., Détienne, F., and Visser, W. (1998). Measuring cognitive activities in software engineering. The 20th International Conference on Software Engineering (ICES98). Kyoto, Japan. April 19–25.

Rosch, E. (1978) Principles of categorization, in E. Rosch and B. Lloyd (eds), *Cognition and categorization*, pp. 28–49. Laurence Erlbaum Associates, Hillsdale, NJ.

Rosch, E., Mervis, C. B., Gray, W., Johnson, D. and Boyes-Braem, P. (1965) Basic objects in natural categories. *Cognitive Psychology*, 8, 133–156.

Rosson, M.B. and Alpert, S.R. (1990) The cognitive consequences of object-oriented design. *Human-Computer Interaction*, 5, 345–379.

Rosson, M.B. and Carroll, J.M. (1993) Active programming strategies in reuse. Proceedings of ECOOP'93, *Object-Oriented Programming*, pp. 4–18. Springer-Verlag, Berlin.

Rosson, M. B., and Gold, E. (1989) Problem-solution mapping in object-oriented design. Research Report IBM, RC 14496.

Rouanet, J. and Gateau, Y. (1967) Le travail du programmeur de gestion: essai de description. AFPA-CERP, Paris.

Rouet, J-F., Deleuze-Dordron, C. and Bisseret, A. (1995a) Documentation skills in novice and expert programmers: an empirical comparison. Proceedings of the seventh workshop of the Psychology of Programming Interest Group (PPIG), 4–6 January 1995. Edinburgh, Scotland.

Rouet, J-F., Deleuze-Dordron, C. and Bisseret, A. (1995b) Documentation as part of design: exploratory field studies, in K. Nordby, P.H. Helmersen, D.J. Gilmore and S.A. Arnesen (eds): Proceedings of INTERACT'95. Chapman and Hall. 213–216.

Rumelhart, D.E. and Norman, D. (1978) Accretion, tuning and restructuring: three modes of learning, in J.W. Cotton and R. Klatsky (eds), *Semantic factors in cognition*. Laurence Erlbaum Associates Inc., Hillsdale, NJ

Rumelhart, D.E. (1981) Understanding understanding. Report, Center for Human Information Processing, University of California, San Diego, CA.

Sauvagnac, C., Falzon, P., and Leblond, R. (1997) La mémoire organisationnelle: reconstruction du passé, construction du futur. Actes des journées *Ingénieries de la connaissance*, Roscoff, 20–22 Mai 1997. Rocquencourt: INRIA.

Schank, R. and Abelson, R. (1977) Scripts-Plans-Goals and Understanding. Hillsdale, N.J.: Lawrence Erlbaum Associates.

Schmalhofer, F. and Glavanov, D. (1986) Three Components of Understanding a Programmer's Manual: Verbatim, Propositional, and Situational Representations. *Journal of Memory and Language*, 25, pp. 279–294.

Scholtz, J. and Wiedenbeck, S. (1990a) Learning second and subsequent programming languages: a problem of transfer. *International Journal of Human-Computer Interaction*, 2(1), 51–57.

Scholtz, J. and Wiedenbeck, S. (1990b) Learning to Program in Another Language, in D. Diaper, D. Gilmore, G. Cockton and B. Shackel (eds), *Human Computer Interaction, Proceedings of INTERACT '90*, pp 925–930. North Holland, Amsterdam.

Scholtz, J. and Wiedenbeck, S. (1993). An analysis of novice programmers learning a second language. In C. R. Cook, J. C. Scholtz, and J. C. Spohrer (eds), *Empirical Studies of Programmers: Fifth Workshop*, pp. 187–205. Ablex Publishing Corporation, Norwood, NJ.

Schroeder, A. (1983) Outils de mesures de programmes. Bulletin du groupe de travail *génie logiciel* de l'AFCET-informatique (Mai 1983), pp. 91–98.

Shaft, T. M. and Vessey, I. (1995) The relevance of Application domain knowledge: the case of computer program comprehension. *Information Systems Research*, 6(3), 286–299.

Sharp, H. (1991) The role of domain knowledge in software design. *Behaviour and Information Technology*, 10(5), 383–401.

Sheil, B. (1981) The psychological study of programming. *ACM Computing Surveys*, 13(1), 101–120.

Sheppard, S. B., Curtis, B., Milliman, P. and Love, T. (1979) Modern coding practices and programmer performance. *Computer*, 12 (2), 41–49.

Sheppard, S. B., Curtis, B., Milliman, P., Borst, M. A. and Love, T. (1979) First-year results from a research program on human factors in software engineering. *Proceeding of the National Computer Conference*, New York, USA, pp. 1021–1027. AFIPS Press, Montvale.

Shneiderman, B. (1976). Exploratory experiments in programmer behaviour. *International Journal of Computer and Information Sciences*, 5(2), 123–143.

Shneiderman, B. (1980) Software Psychology. Human factors in computer and information systems. Winthrop Publishers, Cambridge, MA.

Shneiderman, B., Mayer, R., McKay, D. and Heller, P. (1977). Experimental investigations of the utility of detailed flowcharts in programming. *Communications of the ACM*, 20, 373–381.

Siddiqi, J., Osborne, R., Roast, C. and Khazaei, B. (1996). The pitfalls of changing paradigms, in W.D. Gray, and D.A. Boehm-Davis (eds), *Empirical Studies of Programmers: Sixth Workshop* 5-7 January 1996, Washington DC. US, pp. 219–232, Ablex Publishing Corporation, Norwood, NJ.

Sime, M. E., Green, T. R. G. and Guest, D.J. (1973). Psychological evaluation of two conditional constructions used in computer languages. *International Journal of Man-Machine Studies*, 5, 105–113.

Sime, M. E., Green, T. R. G. and Guest, D.J. (1977) Scope marking in computer conditionals: a psychological evaluation. *International Journal of Man-Machine Studies, 9,* 107–118.

Singer, J., and Lethbridge, T. (1998) Studying work practices to assist tool design in software engineering. *Proceedings of the Sixth International Workshop on Program Comprehension (IWPC'98),* pp. 173–179, IEEE Computer Society.

Soloway, E. (1986) What to do next: meeting the challenge of programming-in-the-large, in E. Soloway and S. Iyengar (eds), *Empirical Studies of Programmers.* Proceeding of the First Workshop on Empirical Studies of Programmers, pp. 263–268. Ablex Publishing Corporation, Norwood, NJ.

Soloway, E. and Ehrlich, K. (1984) Empirical Studies of Programming Knowledge. *IEEE Transactions on Software Engineering,* SE-10(5), 595–609.

Soloway, E., Ehrlich, K. and Bonar, J. (1982a) Tapping into Tacit Programming Knowledge. *Human Factors in Computer Systems,* 15–17, 52–57.

Soloway, E., Ehrlich, K., Bonar, J. and Greenspan, J. (1982b) What do novices know about programming? in A. Badre and B. Shneiderman (eds): *Directions in human computer interaction.* Ablex Publishing corporation, Norwood, NJ.

Soloway, E., Pinto, J., Letovsky, S., Littman, D. and Lampert, R. (1988) Designing documentation to compensate for delocalized plans. *Communications of the ACM,* 31(11), 1259–1267.

Sonnentag, S. (1995) Excellent software professionals: experience, work activities, and perception by peers. *Behaviour and Information Technology,* 14 (5), 289–299.

Sonnentag, S. (1996) Knowledge about working strategies and errors in software professionals: effects of expertise and experience, in P. Vanneste, K. Bertels, B. de Decker and J-M. Jaques (eds), *Proceedings of the Eighth Workshop the Psychology of Programming Interest Group,* 10–12 April, pp. 164–166, Ghent, Belgium.

Sunohara, T., Takano, A., Uehara, K. and Ohkawa. T. (1981) Program complexity measure for software development management. *Proceedings of the Fifth International Conference on Software Engineering,* 9–12 March, pp. 100–106, San Diego, CA.

Teasley, B. E. (1994) The effects of naming style and expertise on program comprehension. *International Journal of Human-Computer Studies,* 40, 757–770.

Tilley, S. R. (1998) Coming attractions in program understanding II: highlights of 1997 and opportunities for 1998. Technical report CMU/SEI-98-TR-001. Software Engineering Institute, Carnegie Mellon University, Pittsburgh, PA.

Trabasso, T. and Suh, S. (1993) Understanding text: achieving explanatory coherence through on-line inferences and mental operations in working memory. *Discourse Processes,* 16, 3–34.

Tracz, W. (1987). Software reuse: motivators and inhibitors. In *Compcon '87,* pp. 358–363, 32nd IEEE Computer Society International Conference, San Francisco.

van Dijk, T.A. and Kintsch, W. (1983) *Strategies of Discourse Comprehension.* Academic Press, New York.

van Hillegersberg, J., Kumar, K. and Welke, R.J. (1995) Maintenance of object-oriented systems: an empirical analysis of the performance and strategies of programmers new to object-oriented techniques. Proceedings of PPIG7, University of Edinburgh, 4–6 January.

Vessey, I. (1989) Towards a theory of computer program bugs: an empirical test. *International Journal of Man-Machine Studies,* 30, 23–46.

Visser, W. (1987) Strategies in Programming Programmable Controllers: A Field Study on a Professional Programmer, in G. M. Olson, S. Sheppard and E. Soloway, *Empirical Studies of Programmers*: Second Workshop, pp. 217–230. Ablex Publishing Corporation, Norwood, NJ.

Visser, W. (1994a) Planning and organization in expert design activities, in D. Gilmore, R. Winder and F. Détienne (eds), *User Centred Requirements for Software Engineering Environments,* pp. 25–40, NATO ASI Series, Springer-Verlag.

Visser, W. (1994b) Organization of design activities: opportunistic, with hierarchical episodes. *Interacting with Computers,* 6 (3), 239–274.

Visser, W. and Hoc, J.-M. (1990). Expert software design strategies, in J.-M. Hoc, T. R. G. Green, R. Samurçay, and D. Gilmore (eds), *Psychology of Programming,* pp. 235–250. Academic Press, London.

Visser, W. and Trousse, B. (1993). Reuse of designs: desperately seeking an interdisciplinary cognitive approach, in W. Visser (ed.), *Proceedings of the Workshop of the Thirteenth International Joint Conference on Artificial Intelligence Reuse of designs: an interdisciplinary cognitive approach,* pp. 1–14, 29 August, 1993, INRIA Rocquencourt, Chambery.

Von Mayrhauser, A. and Vans, A. M. (1998) Program understanding behavior during adaptation of large scale software. *Proceedings of the Sixth International Workshop on Program Comprehension (IWPC'98),* pp. 164–172, IEEE Computer Society.

Vosniadou, S., and Ortony, A. (1989) *Similarity and Analogical Reasoning.* Cambridge University Press, New York.

Walker, W. H., and Kintsch, W. (1985). Automatic and Strategic Aspects of Knowledge Retrieval. *Cognitive Science,* 9, 261–283.

Weissman, L. (1974) Psychological complexity of computer programs: an experimental methodology. ACM SIGPLAN Notices, 9.

Widowski, D. and Eyferth, K. (1986) Representation of computer programs in memory. Proceeding of the Third European Conference on Cognitive Ergonomics, 15–19 September, Paris, France.

Wiedenbeck, S. (1985) Novice expert differences in programming skills. *International Journal of Man-Machine Studies*, 23, 383–390.

Wiedenbeck, S. (1986a) Processes in Computer Program Comprehension. In E. Soloway and S. Iyengar (eds), *Empirical Studies of Programmers: First Workshop*, pp. 48–57. Ablex Publishing Corporation, Norwood, NJ.

Wiedenbeck, S. (1986b) Beacons in computer program comprehension. *International Journal of Man-Machine Studies*, 25, 697–709.

Wiedenbeck, S., Fix, V. and Scholtz, J. (1993) Characteristics of the mental representation of novice and expert programmers: an empirical study. Internal *Journal of Man Machine Studies*, 39, 793–812.

Wirth, N. (1974) On the composition of well-structured programs. *Computing Surveys*, 6, 247–259.

Wirth, N. (1976) Algorithms + data structures = programs. Prentice Hall, Englewood Cliffs, NJ.

Woodfield, S.N., Embley, D.W. and Scott, D.T. (1987) Can programmers reuse software? *IEEE Software*, (July 1987), pp. 52–59.

Wright, P. (1977) Presenting technical information: a survey of research findings. *Instructional Science*, 6, 93–134.

Wu, Q. and Anderson, J.R. (1991) Knowledge Transfer among Programming Languages, *Proceedings of the 13th Conference of the Cognitive Science Society*, pp. 376–381. Laurence Erlbaum Associates Inc., Hillsdale, NJ.

Zwaan, R.A., Magliano, J.P. and Graesser, A.C. (1995) Dimensions of situation model construction in narrative comprehension. Journal of Experimental Psychology: Learning, Memory and Cognition, 21(2), 386–397.

Index

PRACTITIONER SERIES

Series Editor: Ray Paul
Editorial Board: Frank Bott, Nic Holt,
                   Kay Hughes, Elizabeth Hull,
                   Richard Nance, Russel Winder and Sion Wyn

These books are written by practitioners for practitioners.

They offer thoroughly practical hands-on advice on how to tackle specific problems. So, if you are already a practitioner in the development, exploitation or management of IS/IT systems, or you need to acquire an awareness and knowledge of principles and current practice in an IT/IS topic fast then these are the books for you.

All books in this series will be clear, concise and problem solving and will cover a wide range of areas including:
- systems design techniques
- performance modelling
- cost and estimation control
- software maintenance
- quality assurance
- database design and administration
- HCI
- safety critical systems
- distributed computer systems
- internet and web applications
- communications, networks and security
- multimedia, hypermedia and digital libraries
- object technology
- client-server
- formal methods
- design approaches
- IT management

All books are, of course, available from all good booksellers (who can order them even if they are not in stock), but if you have difficulties you can contact the publishers direct, by telephoning +44 (0) 1483 418822 (in the UK & Europe), +1/212/4 60/15 00 (in the USA), or by emailing orders@svl.co.uk

www.springer.de www.springer-ny.com